Internet Explorer 5
explained

Books Available

By both authors:
BP327 DOS one step at a time
BP337 A Concise User's Guide to Lotus 1-2-3 for Windows
BP341 MS-DOS explained
BP346 Programming in Visual Basic for Windows
BP352 Excel 5 explained
BP362 Access one step at a time
BP387 Windows one step at a time
BP388 Why not personalise your PC
BP400 Windows 95 explained
BP406 MS Word 95 explained
BP407 Excel 95 explained
BP408 Access 95 one step at a time
BP409 MS Office 95 one step at a time
BP415 Using Netscape on the Internet*
BP420 E-mail on the Internet*
BP426 MS-Office 97 explained
BP428 MS-Word 97 explained
BP429 MS-Excel 97 explained
BP430 MS-Access 97 one step at a time
BP433 Your own Web site on the Internet
BP448 Lotus SmartSuite 97 explained
BP456 Windows 98 explained*
BP460 Using Microsoft Explorer 4 on the Internet*
BP464 E-mail and News with Outlook Express*
BP465 Lotus SmartSuite Millennium explained
BP471 Microsoft Office 2000 explained
BP472 Microsoft Word 2000 explained
BP473 Microsoft Excel 2000 explained
BP474 Microsoft Access 2000 explained
BP478 Microsoft Works 2000 explained
BP486 Using Linux the easy way*
BP488 Internet Explorer 5 explained*

By Noel Kantaris:
BP258 Learning to Program in C
BP259 A Concise Introduction to UNIX*
BP284 Programming in QuickBASIC
BP325 A Concise User's Guide to Windows 3.1

Internet Explorer 5 explained

by

P.R.M. Oliver
and
N. Kantaris

Bernard Babani (publishing) Ltd
The Grampians
Shepherds Bush Road
London W6 7NF
England

Please Note

Although every care has been taken with the production of this book to ensure that any projects, designs, modifications and/or programs, etc., contained herewith, operate in a correct and safe manner and also that any components specified are normally available in Great Britain, the Publishers and Author(s) do not accept responsibility in any way for the failure (including fault in design) of any project, design, modification or program to work correctly or to cause damage to any equipment that it may be connected to or used in conjunction with, or in respect of any other damage or injury that may be so caused, nor do the Publishers accept responsibility in any way for the failure to obtain specified components.

Notice is also given that if equipment that is still under warranty is modified in any way or used or connected with home-built equipment then that warranty may be void.

© 2000 BERNARD BABANI (publishing) LTD

First Published - May 2000

British Library Cataloguing in Publication Data:

A catalogue record for this book is available from the
British Library

ISBN 0 85934 488 6

Cover Design by Gregor Arthur
Printed and Bound in Great Britain by Bath Press

About this Book

Internet Explorer 5 explained has been written to help you get to grips with the Internet and e-mail in general and with browsing, or surfing, the Web with Microsoft's Internet Explorer in particular.

These days you can't read a paper, listen to the radio, or watch television very long before you hear or see mention of the Internet. It has become an integral part of our lives over the last few years. What importance will it have after the next few years? If it follows the current trend and carries on growing exponentially, it could well become the most important technical development in the history of mankind. So as not to get completely left behind we feel that everyone should test the water, but beware, the Web can be very habit forming!

An attempt has been made not to use too much 'jargon', but with this subject, some is inevitable, so a fairly detailed glossary of terms is included, which should be used with the text where necessary.

The book starts by overviewing the short history of the Internet (from the US military to rampant commercialism) and describes how the Web fits into the general scene.

A chapter follows explaining how you can obtain and install Explorer 5 on your PC. How to go about connecting to the Internet and obtaining the technical help that may be needed is also very briefly covered. The book was written using version 5.5 of the Internet Explorer, working on a PC under the Windows 98 operating system.

Internet Explorer 5 explained

The following chapters describe this version of Internet Explorer and how best to use it for surfing the Web. Using Outlook Express 5 for handling your e-mail and your Newsgroup activities then follows.

Chapters are included on how to find your way around the Web using some of the many search 'engines' that are available, and how to recognise and guard against some of the unfortunate behaviour traits that have developed with the Internet.

One thing to remember when reading the book is that the whole Internet scenario is changing every day, especially the World Wide Web. What is there to look at today, may have gone, or changed shape, by tomorrow.

The book does not describe how to set up your PC, or how to use Windows. If you need to know more about the Windows environment, then we suggest you select an appropriate book from the 'Books Available' list - these are all published by BERNARD BABANI (publishing) Ltd.

Like the rest of our computer series, this book was written with the busy person in mind. It is not necessary to learn all there is to know about a subject, when reading a few selected pages can usually do the same thing quite adequately. Using this book, it is hoped that you will be able to come to terms with the Internet, Microsoft Explorer 5, Outlook Express 5 and the Web and get the most out of your computer in terms of efficiency, productivity and enjoyment, and that you will be able to do it in the shortest, most effective and informative way. Good luck.

If you would like to purchase a Companion Disc for any of our books listed on page ii, **apart from this book and the ones marked with an asterisk**, containing the file/program listings which appear in them, then fill in the form at the back of the book and send it to Phil Oliver at the address given.

About the Authors

Phil Oliver graduated in Mining Engineering at Camborne School of Mines in 1967 and since then has specialised in most aspects of surface mining technology, with a particular emphasis on computer related techniques. He has worked in Guyana, Canada, several Middle Eastern and Central Asian countries, South Africa and the United Kingdom, on such diverse projects as: the planning and management of bauxite, iron, gold and coal mines; rock excavation contracting in the UK; international mining equipment sales and international mine consulting. In 1988 he took up a lecturing position at Camborne School of Mines (part of Exeter University) in Surface Mining and Management. He retired from full-time lecturing in 1998, to spend more time consulting, writing, and developing Web sites.

Noel Kantaris graduated in Electrical Engineering at Bristol University and after spending three years in the Electronics Industry in London, took up a Tutorship in Physics at the University of Queensland. Research interests in Ionospheric Physics, led to the degrees of M.E. in Electronics and Ph.D. in Physics. On return to the UK, he took up a Post-Doctoral Research Fellowship in Radio Physics at the University of Leicester, and then in 1973 a lecturing position in Engineering at the Camborne School of Mines, Cornwall, (part of Exeter University), where between 1978 and 1997 he was also the CSM Computing Manager. At present he is IT Director of FFC Ltd.

Acknowledgements

We would like to thank both Microsoft for making this excellent software available free of charge, or commitment, on the Internet, and Future Publishing for supplying it on the CD ROMs that appear with their magazines PC Plus and .Net every month.

Trademarks

Arial and **Times New Roman** are registered trademarks of The Monotype Corporation plc.

HP and LaserJet are registered trademarks of Hewlett Packard Corporation.

IBM is a registered trademark of International Business Machines, Inc.

Intel is a registered trademark of Intel Corporation.

Microsoft, MS-DOS, Windows, Windows NT, and **Visual Basic**, are either registered trademarks or trademarks of Microsoft Corporation.

PostScript is a registered trademark of Adobe Systems Incorporated.

Macintosh, QuickTime and **TrueType** are registered trademarks of Apple Computer, Inc.

All other brand and product names used in the book are recognised as trademarks, or registered trademarks, of their respective companies.

Contents

1. **The Internet** 1
   What is the Internet? - A Brief History 1
   Why Use the Internet? 4
      Surfing the Net 4
      E-mail 4
      Newsgroups 5
      Long Distance Computing 5
      File Transfers 5
   The World Wide Web 5
   HTML - The Original Web Language 7
      How Links are Named 7

2. **Internet Exploring** 9
   Microsoft Products 10
   Computer Hardware 10
   Getting Online 11
   Getting your Software 12
      Installing Internet Explorer 12
   Starting Internet Explorer 14
   Your PC Settings 16
   A Trial Run 17

3. **Basic Program Features** 21
   Explorer Screen Layout 21
   Menu Bar Options 24
      Keyboard Shortcuts 25
   Mouse Right-click Menu 25
   The Standard Toolbar 26
      Customising the Toolbar 28
   The Address Bar 30
   The Links Bar 32
   Fullscreen View 32
   General Option Settings 33
   Saving Pictures 35
   Explorer Help 36
      Another Online Tutorial 38

4. More Skills and Features 39
    A Useful Site 40
    Using Web Information 40
        The Mouse Pointer 41
        Copying Text 41
        Viewing Source Code 42
        Saving a Target Link 42
    Saving Whole Pages 43
        Web Page, Complete (*.htm, *.html) 43
        Web Archive, Single File (*.mht) 44
        Web Page, HTML Only (*.htm, *.html) 44
        Text File (*.txt) 44
    Downloading a Program File 45
        An Internet Software Source 47
    Printing Web Pages 48
        Print Preview 50
    History Files 51
        The Cache 53
    Security 54
        Explorer Security Measures 55
        Security Zones 55
        A Secure Transaction 56
    New Explorer Components 58

5. Where Shall We Go Today? 59
    The Search Assistant 59
        Customising the Assistant 60
    Search Tools 61
    What is Available 62
    Deja.com - As an Example 66

6. Favorites and Working Offline 69
    Favorites 69
        Adding a Favorite 70
        Using Favorites 71
    The Organize Favorites Window 72
    Adding a New Folder 73
        Framed Pages as Favorites 74
        Links Bar Favorites 74

Internet Explorer 5 explained

    Using Explorer Offline 75
        Viewing History Pages Offline 75
        Offline Favorites 75
        Working Offline 78
    Favorite Properties 79

7. E-mail with Outlook Express 5 81

    What is E-mail 81
        E-mail Addresses 82
    Connecting to your Server 84
    A Trial Run 88
    The Main Window 89
        The Folders List 89
        The Contacts Pane 90
        The Message List 90
        Message Status Icons 91
        The Preview Pane 91
        The Main Window Toolbar 92
    The Read Message Window 93
        The Read Message Toolbar 93
        Viewing File Attachments 94
    The New Message Window 94
        Message Stationery 95
        The New Message Toolbar 96
        Your Own Signature 97
        Message Formatting 98
        Adding Attachments 99
    Sending E-mail Messages 100
    Replying to a Message 100
    Removing Deleted Messages 101
    Organising your Messages 101
        The System Folders 102

8. Some Other E-mail Features 103

    Outlook Express Help 103
    Spell Checking 104
    Connection at Start-Up 106
    Printing your Messages 107
    The Address Book 109
        Address Book Help 111

	Using Message Rules	112
	Blocked Senders List	114
	Microsoft Hotmail	115
	Mailing Lists	117
	Finding a Suitable List	117
	Typical Subscription Commands	118
	Often Used E-mail Symbols	119
	Acronyms	119
	Smileys	119

9. News with Outlook Express 5 121

How Usenet Works	121
Usenet Newsgroups	122
Starting to Read News	123
Internet News Configuration	123
The Newsgroup Subscriptions Window	125
Subscribing to a Group	126
The News Window	127
The News Toolbar	128
The Read Message Window	129
Replying to Messages	129
Postings Containing Pictures	130
Threaded Messages	132
Offline Viewing	133
Newsgroup Caches	134
Controlling the Caches	134
On Your Own	136

10. Behaviour on the Internet 137

Internet Flames	137
Spam, Spam, Bacon and Spam	138
Other Usenet Types	138
Some Internet Etiquette	139
Censoring your Web Browser	141
Still a Feature for the Future	142

11. Glossary of Terms 143

Appendix A - Keyboard Shortcuts 163
Keyboard Shortcuts for Explorer 5 163
Keyboard Shortcuts for Outlook Express 5 165

Appendix B - Internet File Formats 167
Plain Text (ASCII) Files 167
Formatted Documents 167
Compressed and Encoded Files 168
Graphics Files 169
Sound Files 170
Video Files 170

Index 171

1
The Internet

As long as you have a computer and can access the Internet you can access millions of Web pages and use e-mail for keeping in touch with your friends, family and maybe more important for professional reasons.

There are several packages, most of them freely available now, that make this whole procedure very easy, once you know how. One of our favourites is Microsoft's Explorer 5 Web browser and Outlook Express 5 which comes with it. At the time of writing, this was the most popular browser in use. If your PC has Windows 98, or later, you will already have it; if not, we will point you in the right direction, but first we must set the scene.

What is the Internet? - A Brief History

The universal use of Web sites and e-mail has become possible because of the explosive growth of the Internet in the last decade. So how did this all come about?

In the mid 1960s with the cold war very prominent, the US military faced a strange strategic problem. How could the country successfully communicate after a possible nuclear war? They would need a command and control communication network linking the cities, states and military bases, etc. But, no matter how the network was protected it would always be vulnerable to the impact of a nuclear attack and if the network had a control centre it would be the first to go.

As a solution, the concept was developed that the network itself should be assumed to be unreliable at all times and

The Internet

should be designed to overcome this unreliability. To achieve this, all the nodes (devices attached to the network, which have their own address and use the network as a means of communication) would be equal in status, each with its own authority to originate, pass, and receive messages. The messages themselves would be divided into small parts, or packets, with each being separately addressed. The transmission of each packet of data would begin at a specified source node, and end at another specified destination node, but would find its own way through the network, with the route taken being unimportant. With this concept, if sections of the network were destroyed, that wouldn't matter as the packets would use the surviving parts.

The National Physical Laboratory, here in the UK, set up the first test network on these principles in 1968. Shortly afterwards, the Pentagon's Advanced Research Projects Agency (ARPA) funded a larger, more ambitious project in the USA, with the high-speed 'supercomputers' of the day as the network nodes.

In 1969, the first such node was installed in UCLA. By December of that year, there were four nodes on the infant network, which was named ARPANET, after its sponsor. The four computers could transfer data on dedicated high-speed transmission lines, and could be programmed remotely from the other nodes. For the first time, scientists and researchers could share one another's computer facilities from a long distance. By 1972 there were thirty-seven nodes in ARPANET.

It soon became apparent, however, that much of the traffic on ARPANET was not long-distance computing, but consisted of news and personal messages. Researchers were using ARPANET not only to collaborate on projects and to exchange ideas on work, but to socialise. They had their own personal accounts on the ARPANET computers, and their own personal addresses for electronic mail and they were very enthusiastic about this particular new service, which we now know as e-mail.

Throughout the 70s, the ARPA network grew, its decentralised structure making expansion easy as it could accommodate different types of computers, as long as they could speak the standard packet-switching language. ARPA's original standard for communication was known as NCP short for 'Network Control Protocol', but this was soon superseded by the higher-level standard known as TCP/IP, which has survived until today.

TCP, or 'Transmission Control Protocol', converts messages into streams of packets at the source, then reassembles them back into messages at the destination. IP, or 'Internet Protocol', handles the addressing.

Over the years, ARPANET itself became a smaller and smaller part of the growing proliferation of other networked machines, but TCP/IP continued to link them all. As the 70s and 80s advanced, many different groups found themselves in possession of powerful computers. It was fairly easy to link these computers to the growing global network. As the use of TCP/IP, which was in the public domain by that time, became more common, entire other networks were incorporated into the **Internet**.

In 1984 the National Science Foundation became involved and created the new NSFNET linking newer and faster supercomputers with bigger and faster links. Other US government agencies joined the bandwagon, including NASA, the National Institutes of Health, and the Department of Energy.

ARPANET itself formally died in 1989, but its functions not only continued but were steadily improved. In Europe, major international 'backbone' networks started to provide connectivity to many millions of computers on a large number of other networks. Commercial network providers in both the US, Europe and Asia were beginning to offer Internet access and support on a competitive basis to any interested parties. In fact the extended use of the Internet cost the original founders little or nothing extra, since each new node was independent, and had to handle its own technical requirements and funding.

Now in the new century there are millions of nodes in the Internet, scattered throughout the world, with more coming on-line all the time and many more millions of people using this often named 'Information Super Highway' every day.

Built to be indestructible and with no centralised control, it's no wonder the word 'anarchistic' is often bandied around when the Internet is discussed!

Why Use the Internet?

Now we know what the Internet is, what can we use it for? Basically, five things spring to mind; two are the reason for this book, and the other three are mentioned briefly for completeness:

- Browsing, or surfing the Net.
- Sending and receiving e-mail messages.
- Taking part in News, or discussion groups.
- Accessing data stored on distant computers.
- Transferring data and program files from and to these distant computers.

Surfing the Net

The World Wide Web, or Web as we shall call it, consists of client computers (yours and mine) and server computers which handle multimedia documents with 'hypertext' links built into them. Clicking the links on a page in a Web browser on your PC, like Internet Explorer, brings documents located on a distant server to your screen, irrespective of the server's geographic location. Documents may contain text, images, sounds, movies, interactive programs (scripts), or a combination of these, in other words - multimedia. Surfing the Web just means moving from site to site and following the links that catch your eye.

E-mail

Electronic mail, has to be one of the main uses of the Internet. It is very much faster that letter mail, which is known as 'snailmail' by regular e-mail users. It consists of electronic text, that is transmitted, sometimes in seconds, to anywhere else in the World that is connected to a main network. E-mail can also be used to send software and other types of files which are 'attached' to your message. As we shall see in later chapters, modern software such as Outlook Express makes this a very easy process.

Newsgroups

Discussion groups, or 'newsgroups', are another feature of the Internet that are easily accessed with Outlook Express. On the Internet they are generally known as USENET and consist of many, many thousands of separate groups which let you freely participate in discussions on a vast number of subjects.

Long Distance Computing

Using a program like Telnet you can maintain accounts on distant computers, run programs from them as if they were on your own PC, and generally make use of powerful supercomputers a continent away.

File Transfers

There is a fantastic amount of free software available over the Internet, as well as a multitude of text and graphics files on almost any subject you care to mention.

File transfers carried out with a protocol known as FTP, allow Internet users to access remote machines and retrieve these for their own use.

The World Wide Web

Up until a few years ago all of these activities required very expensive computing facilities and a large measure of computer literacy. Times have changed, however, and it is now possible to very easily and cheaply install a modem in your PC, connect to the Internet and with a Web browser, like

The Internet

Microsoft's Internet Explorer 5, carry them out with very little technical knowledge. Hence the reason for this book, to help you on your way.

The World Wide Web, WWW, W3, or Web as we shall call it, was initially developed in Switzerland by CERN (the European Laboratory for Particle Physics), to form a distributed hypermedia system. It now consists of Web client computers (yours and mine) and server computers handling multimedia documents with hypertext links built into them. Client computers use browser software (like Internet Explorer) to view pages of these documents, one at a time. Server computers use Web server software to maintain the documents for us to access.

If you have used the Help pages of Windows you are familiar with a hypertext document. It contains links that you click with the mouse pointer to jump to other information. The advantage of hypertext in a Web document is that if you want more information about a particular subject, you just click on it and another page is opened for you to read or look at. In fact, documents can be linked to other documents (or graphics) by completely different authors and stored in completely different computers; much like footnoting, but you can get the referenced document instantly!

So, to access the Web, you run a browser program, in our case Microsoft Explorer 5, which reads files and documents, and fetches them from other sources on the Internet into the memory of your PC.

So Web browsers, like Explorer, provide users of computer networks with a consistent means to access a variety of media in a very simplified fashion. They have changed the way people view and create information, and have formed the first true global 'hypermedia' network. No wonder their use has taken off so dramatically in the last two years. Hypermedia is a superset of hypertext - it is any medium with pointers to other media. This means that the latest browsers display formatted text, images, play sound clips, or even video type animations. Some of these, however, may require extra hardware, like a sound card, in your computer.

HTML - The Original Web Language

You may never get involved with this, but most Web documents are still created by authors using a language called HTML (HyperText Markup Language). This offers short codes, or tags, to designate graphical elements and hypertext links. Clicking a link on a Web page in your browser, brings documents located on a distant server to your screen, irrespective of the server's geographic location. Documents may contain text, images, sounds, movies, or a combination of these, in other words - multimedia.

How Links are Named

Every link in a hypertext Web document has to have a unique address and for you to use your browser properly you should understand these addresses, or Uniform Resource Locators, (URLs for short). It is possible to represent nearly any file or service on the Internet with a URL and several examples are given below.

The first part of the URL (before the two slashes) specifies the method of access, as described on the next page. The second is typically the domain name of the computer on which the data, or service, is located. Further parts may specify the names of folders and files, the port to connect to, or the text to search for in a database. A URL is always a single unbroken line with **no spaces**.

Here are some examples of URLs:

http://www.ex.ac.uk/location/book.html

This would connect to an HTTP server (in this case a Web server at the University of Exeter) and would retrieve an HTML file (a Web file).

ftp://www.xerox.com/pub/file.txt

This would open an FTP connection to www.xerox.com and retrieve a text file.

file://www.ex.ac.uk/location/pic.gif

This would retrieve a picture file and display it.

The Internet

file://www.ex.ac.uk/location/

This would display the directory contents of a distant location.

news:alt.sex

This would read the latest Usenet news by connecting to a specified news host and would return the articles in the alt.sex newsgroup in hypermedia format.

The first part of the URL (before the two slashes) gives the method of access at that address, as follows:

- **http** - a hypertext document or directory.
- **Gopher** - a gopher document or menu.
- **ftp** - a file available for downloading or a directory of such files.
- **news** - a newsgroup.
- **Telnet** - a computer system that you can log into from across the Internet.
- **WAIS** - a database or document on a WAIS (**W**ide **A**rea **I**nformation **S**earch) database.
- **file** - a file located on a local drive (like your hard drive).

Sites that run Web servers are typically named with a www. at the beginning of the network address. As we shall see, Microsoft Explorer allows you to specify a URL and thus connect to that document, or service. When selecting hypertext links in a Web page, you are actually sending a request to open a URL. In this way, hyperlinks can be made not only to other texts and media, but also to other network services. Web browsers are not simply Web clients, but are also full FTP, Gopher, and Telnet clients in their own rights.

All of these features are now easily available over ordinary phone lines, once you get direct Internet access through a local Internet Service Provider (ISP), as explained in the next chapter.

2

Internet Exploring

At the time of writing this book, the Web browser market for Windows PCs had two main players, Microsoft and Netscape. It is now the practice that browsers are given away free of charge by both these companies. In fact, to establish its dominant position in the market, Microsoft has given away all its browser products, as well as including Explorer as part of the latest Windows, Office and Works packages.

These companies originally rushed to give away very high quality software because they saw a lot of money to be made in the future. By flooding the market with their Navigator software, Netscape were able to float their company on the US stock market in record time and saw its stock price rocket to rather excessive heights. This without making a profit until after it went public and with what looked like a very unimpressive balance sheet. The fact that at the time it was the dominant player in the Internet market was enough for Wall Street and the financial world. The situation now is very different, as Netscape could not survive Microsoft's tactics without being taken over, and they now form part of the AOL empire. But Internet shares in general are still very bullish.

Microsoft have made a habit of dominating their markets. Look at DOS, Windows and then the applications like Excel and Word, etc. The Web browser market went the same way. At the time of writing 60 - 70% of the people who visit our Web sites now use a version of Explorer, much more than those using Netscape's products.

We hope there will be enough room for both of these two major players. Having used both of their current browsers, we feel that Microsoft's version 5 is definitely technically ahead, but having said that, there are features in both that we like. As usual, nothing is perfect!

Microsoft Products

At the time of writing, Microsoft have versions of their Internet Explorer 5 available for use on all the popular Windows operating systems. This book was written using version 5.5 which is the version expected to be shipped with the eventual 'replacement' for Windows 98. As well as including it with this latest version of Windows, Microsoft offers Internet Explorer 5 for the Windows 3.1, Windows 95, and Windows NT/2000 platforms.

Computer Hardware

First, you obviously need a computer! We have written this book with the current most common combination in mind - a PC running under Windows 95 or 98.

If you buy a new PC, it will come with at least Windows 98 and with all the software we are concerned with here already installed. In this case you have no problems. Otherwise, the minimum hardware requirements to run Explorer 5 and Outlook Express 5, are a 486DX/66 MHz, or higher, PC with 16 MB of RAM for Windows 95, 32 MB of RAM minimum for Windows NT/2000 (but as much RAM as possible is recommended).

To install the browser alone requires 45 MB of hard disc space, a typical installation needs 70 MB and a full installation requires 111 MB of space. As the installation is actually an upgrading of your version of Windows, most of this disc space must be available on the disc drive that holds the Windows system itself.

Ideally you will need a Pentium PC with as much RAM and hard disc space as you can get your hands on!

You also need a connection to the Internet, via a Modem, Ethernet Card, or ISDN direct digital phone line. A digital ISDN line is faster than a modem connection, but is considerably more expensive, at the moment.

Getting Online

Unless you are lucky enough to have a PC which is connected to a Local Area Network (LAN) which has Internet access, you will need a modem to be able to communicate with the rest of the world. This is a device that converts data so that it can be transmitted over the telephone system.

You will also need to find, and possibly subscribe to, a suitable Internet Service Provider. There are many such providers in the UK. Most can be listed on the Web by accessing the following address:

   http://thelist.internet.com/

and looking under the UK, or wherever else you are based. Another way would be to buy an Internet based PC magazine from your local newsagent and look at the reviews and adverts. Also you could try your friendly neighbourhood computer store, the telephone directory, or possibly adverts in the computer section of your local paper.

The present trend seems to be for new providers to give free Internet access and to pay for the service with advertising or other revenues. Be careful though before committing yourself to one provider as the quality of service can vary considerably. One thing we can't do here is make specific recommendations, but try and find someone who uses the company you decide on, or have a trial period with them.

What you are ideally looking for is **full dial-up SLIP or PPP connection with unlimited WWW access to the Internet**, and this should be possible by dialling a local number to your provider's access point. (SLIP and PPP are only two communication standards that you need to have, but do not need to understand).

The local call access will mean your phone bills should not be excessive, especially if you do your Internet accessing in off-peak times. The unlimited access means you will not pay any extra to your Internet Provider no matter how many hours you spend on line, just your monthly fee, if any.

A service, like that described, can cost in the region of £10 per month, but you can also get it free; there is a lot of competition.

From now on in this book, we assume that you have an active connection to the Internet. Trouble-shooting this is not within our remit!

Getting your Software

If you already have your version of Explorer 5 and Outlook Express 5 up and running on your computer you can skip the rest of this section. If not, you may want to obtain the software. When you are actually connected to the Internet you can download Microsoft's Internet Explorer software absolutely free by clicking this button on their Web site at:

http://www.microsoft.com/windows/ie/

If you are not yet connected, you obviously can't do this, but there is a another way now anyway. Some computer magazines that come with CD-ROMs carry Web browsers on them. Our favourites are *PC Plus* and *.net*, which most months include the latest browsers from both Netscape and Microsoft. With the size of these browsers this can save many hours of valuable time downloading. The saving in your phone bill may well pay for the magazine as well. One thing to remember though with both sources is to select the version of Explorer designed for your operating system.

Installing Internet Explorer

If you download the program, you have the options to have it automatically installed at the same time, or to have the program files saved to your hard disc. In the latter case, simply double-clicking the downloaded **ie5setup.exe** icon, which is placed on your Windows desktop, will start the installation procedure whenever you are ready.

Internet Exploring

From the CD-ROM just follow the instructions and click **Next** to continue. With either method, once you have accepted the licence agreement, the procedure will start with a window similar to ours shown below. If you do not have enough space on your hard disc, you will be told to free up more room and try again. Good luck.

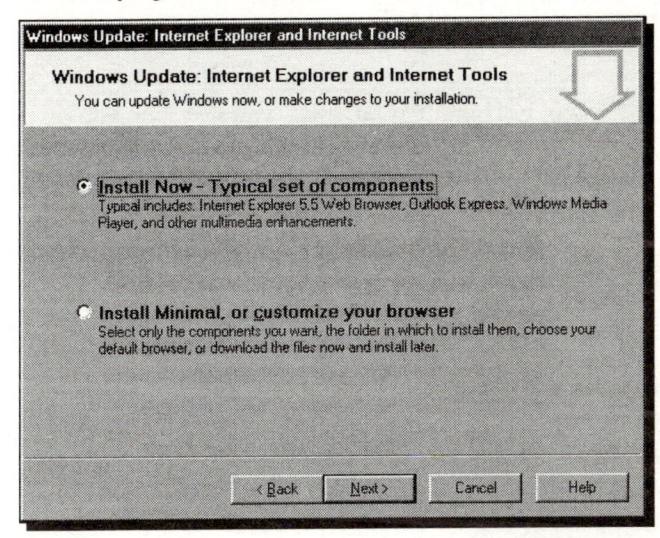

If you want to abort the procedure at any time press the **Cancel** button, but be warned on no account should you then switch off your PC until your old setup is returned. A few minutes of nail biting, hoping there will not be a power cut! The procedure seems to work well, in fact the next time you start the installation procedure it even gives you the option of carrying on from where you last aborted. We accepted this option without any problems.

When you regain control of your PC, you may well find your desktop has changed somewhat, with some new icons added, and the Taskbar will have a Quick Launch bar like that with Windows 98, as shown on the left.

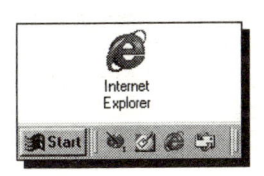

Here two new Explorer icons can be seen, one on the Desktop itself,

2 Internet Exploring

and one on the Quick Launch bar. Clicking either of these will launch the program, as we shall see below. An Outlook Express icon should also have been placed on the bar, unless you opted to install the browser only.

Starting Internet Explorer

Double-clicking the Internet Explorer icon, shown here, will open the browser. The first time you do this it will probably start the Internet Connection Wizard, which steps you through the process of establishing your link to the Internet.

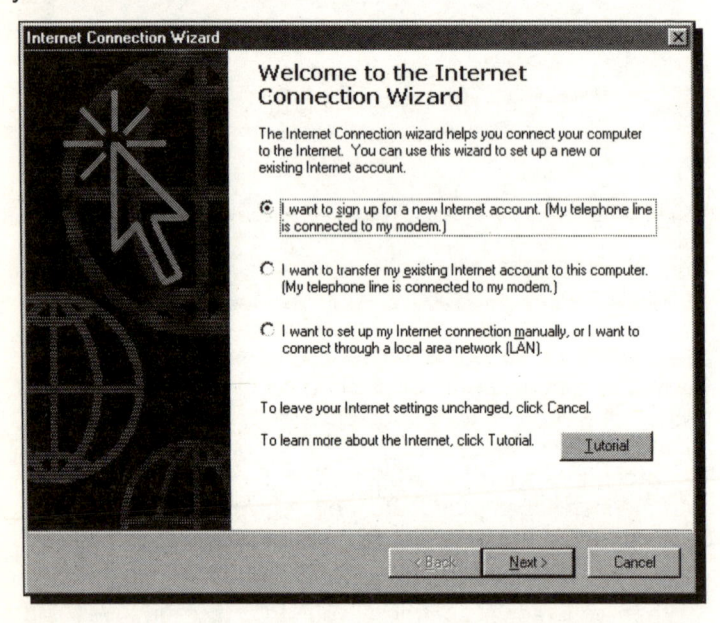

This Wizard can make the process of setting up your connection quite painless. You can open it at any time with the **Tools**, **Internet Options** menu command by clicking the **Setup** button on the **Connections** tabbed sheet. Obviously how you complete the options that are offered will depend on your particular system and circumstances.

Internet Exploring

Before starting this operation be sure to find out from your system administrator or your Internet Service Provider exactly what settings you will need to enter.

After all this procedure you then get your first look at the new browser. If all is well and your Internet connection is open, you may get an opening screen which may look something like that shown above. What actually appears will depend on Microsoft, or your ISP, and will also change very often.

Note that when the Explorer is actually downloading data from the network, the Status Indicator to the right of the menu bar shows with an active display, and the status bar gives an indication of what is actually happening.

The default opening screen shown here is really an advert for MSN, a portal service provided by Microsoft. They would rather you spent all your time working in their territory! You can control what Web page, called your home page, is displayed when you start Explorer, in the **General** settings sheet opened with the **Tools**, **Internet Options** menu command. Select **Use Current** to make the currently open page your home page, or **Use Blank** to show a clear window whenever you start up Explorer.

2 Internet Exploring

Your PC Settings

Before we go any further, a few words on screen display resolutions may be useful. Your computer may well have started life set to a screen resolution of 640 x 480 pixels. It then displays a screen of 640 pixels wide and 480 pixels high on the monitor. The bigger the monitor you have, the bigger the screen resolution you can use, as everything gets smaller as the resolution goes up.

For Web browsing you want as large a resolution as you can get so that you can fit more on the screen. Web pages are almost always too large to fit on one screen. We recommend using a resolution of 800 x 600 if you have a 14" or 15" monitor, and a resolution of 1024 x 768 for 17" and larger monitors.

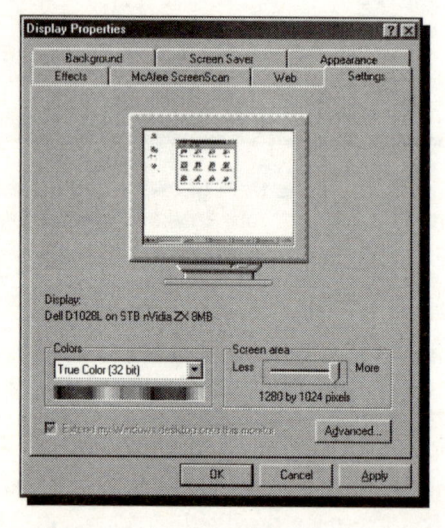

It is easy to change the screen settings, but Windows may have to be re-started for them to take effect. Click the **Start**, button, and then **Settings**, **Control Panel,** double-click on the **Display** icon, and then click the Settings tab to open the window shown here. Another way to open this box is to right-click on the Desktop and select **Properties** from the opened menu. The details above were for one of our PCs,

Internet Exploring 2

yours may well be different. Both the **Colors** and the **Screen area** slider settings are interlinked. The higher the colour setting the lower will be the maximum Desktop area, or resolution. In our case above with a True Colour (32-bit) setting our maximum resolution was 1280 by 1024.

With this colour setting, you get near photographic image quality, and graphics, or pictures, look much better than with only a 256 colour setting. You will find the Web much more entertaining if you surf with thousands, or millions, of colours, instead of just 256.

A Trial Run

You should now be up and running with the Internet Explorer 5, so let's do something. There are many millions of Web pages to look at, so where do we start? You may have started already from the opening page, but there is one UK institution that we all know and love, the Government! They have spent time and money on their Web presentations, so we will take a quick look.

Start Explorer, if it is not already going, and click the Search button, shown here, which is on the button bar known as the Toolbar. Click on **New**, which opens the Search panel on the left of the Explorer window, which should be similar to that shown here.

We will discuss Web searches again in a later chapter, so for now type 'UK Government' in the text box, and click the **Search** button as we did here. In our case, this opened an 'Excite' search page in the panel, and searched for references to the 'UK Government', as shown on the next page. Explorer uses different search engines so your search may not use Excite, but another one. Hopefully the results will be similar!

17

2 Internet Exploring

Excite is just one of the many search utilities, or 'engines' available for finding your way round the Web. It found several relevant Web pages, and brought details of what it considered to be the most relevant ones to the screen. Search tools are very powerful and useful facilities, which we shall discuss further in a later chapter.

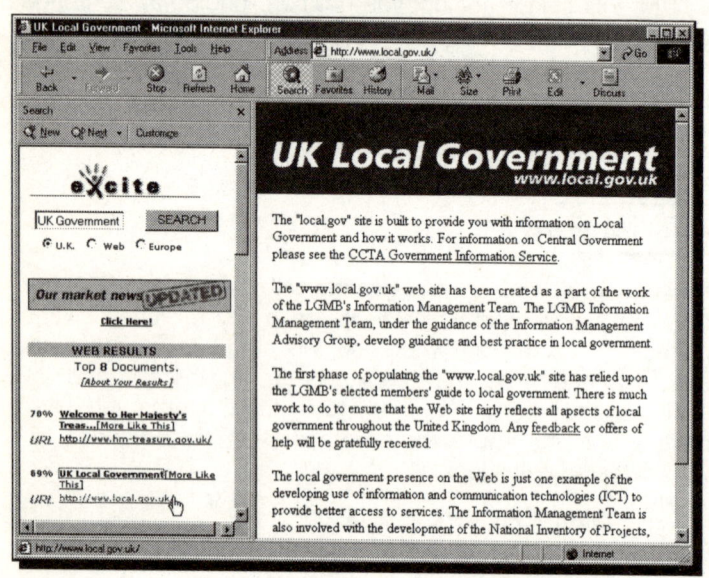

In our case the second entry above will do. Clicking the underlined link UK Local Government opened the home page we were looking for, as shown on the right above.

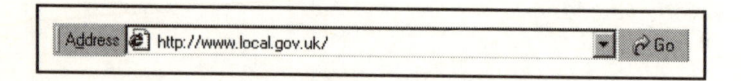

If we had known the URL address (which is also given in the search details) we could have typed it straight into the **Address** bar, as shown above.

This would also have opened the same Web page when the Enter key on the keyboard was pressed, or the **Go** button clicked.

Internet Exploring

Move the mouse pointer over the underlined link <u>CCTA's Government Information Service</u> and when it changes to a 'hand', click the mouse button. This will open the UK Government's main Web site home page, as shown below.

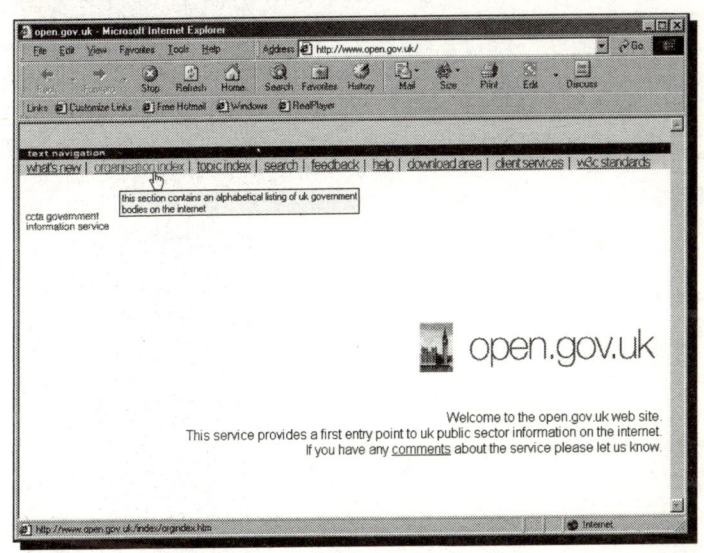

Again try moving the mouse pointer around the screen. When it passes over some of the screen items it changes to a hand, as shown in our illustration. What that means is that each of these graphics is actually a link to another Web page. The status bar, at the bottom of the screen, shows the URL address of the link pointed to, and the banner that opens next to the pointer describes the function of the link. Clicking any of these links on the page will open another page, which may well contain more links.

We will leave it to you to explore this site further. You may find some interesting information, or on the other hand, it may help to send you to sleep. It is not the best looking Web page we have come across, but all the graphics are small and download very quickly. You don't have to make a cup of coffee while you are waiting for it!

2 Internet Exploring

NOTE - If a Web page is taking a long time to load you can open another browser window with the **File**, **New**, **Window** menu command, or the <Ctrl+N> keystroke shortcut. You can have as many Web pages open at the same time as your computer's memory will hold, all doing different things. Be warned though, eventually you will cause a memory overflow and Explorer will lock up. This always seems to happen at the worst possible moment and the only solution is to use the dreaded <Ctrl+Alt+Delete> key combination and shut down the offending program. Sometimes it is even better to re-boot your computer, as this clears all the temporary 'junk' files and settings and lets you start with a clean slate.

3

Basic Program Features

Explorer Screen Layout

The illustration below shows an Explorer 5 window with the four main Toolbars showing, and with the History bar open on the left-hand side.

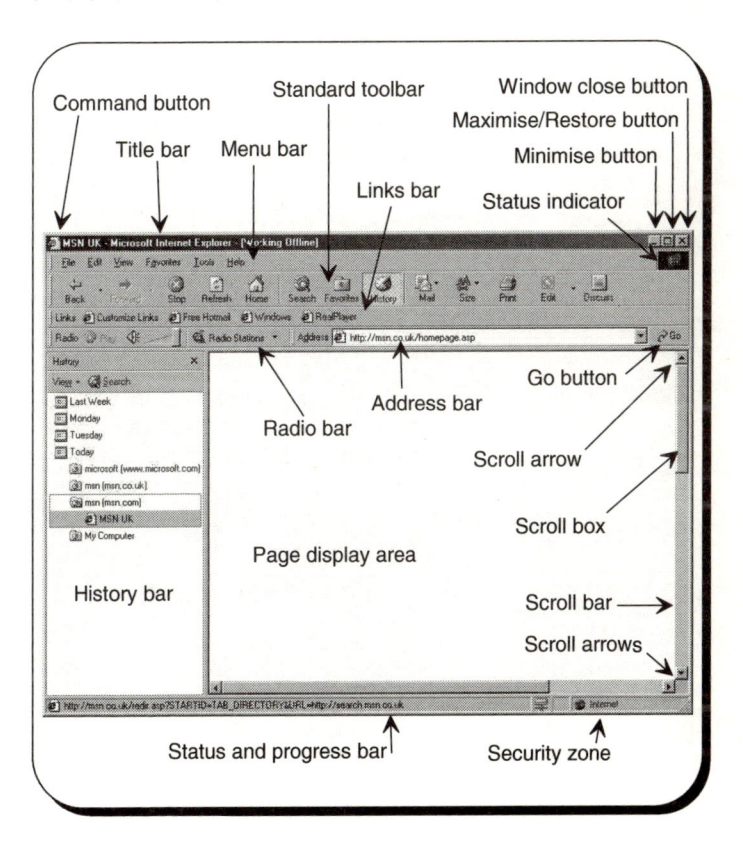

Figure labels: Command button, Title bar, Menu bar, Standard toolbar, Links bar, Window close button, Maximise/Restore button, Minimise button, Status indicator, Radio bar, Address bar, Go button, Scroll arrow, Scroll box, Page display area, History bar, Scroll bar, Scroll arrows, Status and progress bar, Security zone

3 Basic Program Features

It is perhaps worth spending some time looking at the various parts that make up this window, which is subdivided into several areas with the following functions:

Area	*Function*
Command button	Clicking on this program icon button, located in the upper-left corner of each window, displays the pull-down Control menu which can be used to control the window. It includes commands for restoring, maximising, minimising, moving, sizing, and closing the window.
Title bar	The bar which displays the title of the current Web page.
Menu bar	The bar which allows you to choose from several menu options. Clicking on a menu item displays the pull-down menu associated with that item.
Minimise button	The button you point to and click to reduce an application to an icon on the Windows Taskbar at the bottom of the screen.
Restore button	The button you point to and click to restore the window to its former size. When that happens, the Restore button changes to a Maximise button which is used to fill the screen with the active window.
Close button	The X button that you click to close the window.
Standard toolbar	A bar of icons that you click to carry out some of the more common Explorer actions.

Basic Program Features

Address bar	Shows the location of the current page, or the URL of the new page to go to next.
Links bar	Links which automatically load on-line Web pages and can be set up with your own favourites.
Radio bar	Lets you easily control on-line radio stations. Only available if you have installed the Windows Media Player.
Status indicator	Rotates when data transfer is taking place.
Page display	The main body of the window that displays Web pages.
Explorer bars	Vertical bars in the left side of the browser window that open when the Search, Favorites and History Toolbar buttons are actioned. (The History bar is shown on the previous page).
Scroll bars	If the contents of a window will not fit in it, scroll bars are added to the right and/or the bottom of the window.
Scroll arrows	The arrowheads at each end of a scroll bar which you can click to scroll the screen up and down, or left and right.
Scroll box	Dragging this box up or down the scroll bar will rapidly scroll through a Web page.
Status bar	The animated bar that shows the progress of a downloading operation, the address of the link or graphic, pointed to by the mouse, and other status messages.
Security zone	Shows the security settings for the Web site being accessed.

3 Basic Program Features

As is now becoming a standard feature with Microsoft programs, at first glance an empty Explorer window can look a little grey and lifeless, but when you move the mouse pointer over the toolbar its buttons 'light up' when they are active. This is a very pleasing feature, the window being designed not to detract from the Web pages being viewed in it.

Menu Bar Options

Each option on the menu bar has associated with it a pull-down sub-menu. This follows the normal Windows convention, so to access the menu, either click the mouse on an option, or press the <Alt> key, which causes the first option of the menu (in this case **File**) to be highlighted, then use the arrow keys to highlight any of the options in the menu. Pressing either the <Enter> key, or the left mouse button, reveals the pull-down sub-menu of the highlighted menu option. The sub-menu of the **File** option is shown here.

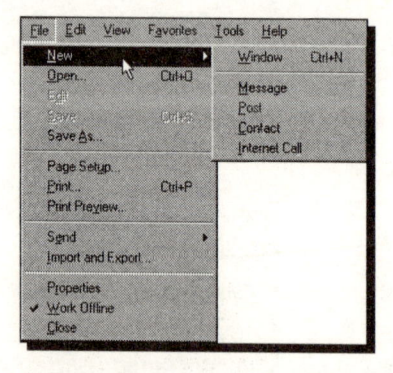

Menu options can also be activated directly by pressing the <Alt> key followed by the underlined letter of the required option. Thus pressing <Alt+F>, also opens the sub-menu of **File**.

You can use the up and down arrow keys to move the highlighted bar up and down a sub-menu, or the right and left arrow keys to move along the options in the Menu bar.

Basic Program Features 3

Pressing the <Enter> key selects the highlighted option or executes the highlighted command. Pressing the <Esc> key once, closes the pull-down sub-menu, while pressing the <Esc> key for a second time, closes the Menu system.

Note that those commands which are not available at any specific time will be inactive and appear on the menu in a lighter colour. In our example on the previous page the option **Save** is not available.

Keyboard Shortcuts

Some of the menu options have keyboard shortcuts attached to them. These are very useful to people who are more used to the keyboard than the mouse. In the **File** sub-menu there are several. For example, pressing <Ctrl+N>, the 'N' key with the 'Ctrl' key also depressed, will open a new browser window.

We have listed the available shortcuts in Appendix A.

Mouse Right-click Menu

You can use your right mouse button to click objects on a page and see a drop-down shortcut, or context, menu, with contents that depend on what you click:

On a link	The menu items refer to the page specified by the link.
On an image	They refer to the image file specified by the image.
On background	They apply to the current page, its text, or its background image.
On the Title bar	They allow you to control the current window.
On the Toolbar	The menu items help you customise the Toolbar area.

25

3 Basic Program Features

This example shows the options that were available when the mouse was right-clicked on the photograph.

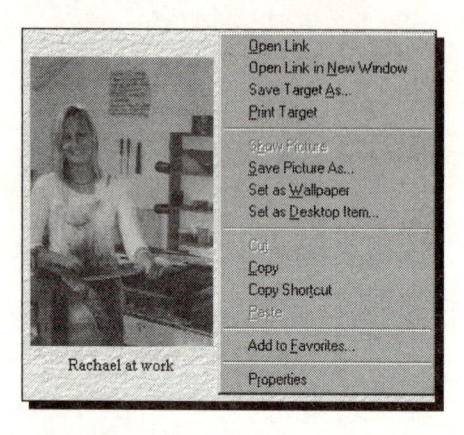

The actions available were: Opening the page linked to the image in the current window, or in a new one, saving the linked page to a file on disc, or sending it to the printer; saving the picture to a file on disc, setting it as the Windows wallpaper or an item on the Windows' desktop; copying the image or its URL to the clipboard; and adding the linked file to the Favorites list. Clicking on **Properties** would show details of the image file.

As usual, unavailable options are shown in grey.

The Standard Toolbar

Most Windows applications are now fully equipped with a Toolbar option, and Internet Explorer is no exception. It contains a series of buttons that you can click with your mouse pointer to quickly carry out a program function.

Most of the button functions are pretty self-explanatory and are as follows:

Basic Program Features 3

Button	*Function*
Back	Displays the previous page viewed, or selects from the drop-down history list.
Forward	Displays the next page on the history list.
Stop	Halts any on-line transfer of page data.
Refresh	Brings a fresh copy of the current Web page to the viewer.
Home	Displays your specified home page, with a Microsoft page as the default.
Search	Opens the Search bar with access to Microsoft selected search facilities.
Favorites	Opens the Favorites bar with access to your saved favourite sites, or bookmarks.
History	Opens the History bar and displays a hierarchical list of the Web pages you have previously viewed. You can browse through these again in Offline mode.
Mail	Gives quick access to your e-mail and Newsgroup facilities.
Size	Gives a choice of 5 font sizes for the browser to use.
Print	Prints the open Web page, or frame, using the current print settings.
Edit	Opens the current Web page in one of the available HTML editors on your system.
Discuss	Gives you access to discussion groups, or opens a wizard for you to set one up.

If the Toolbar is not showing when a window is opened, you simply open the **View** menu, select the **Toolbars** option and choose what features you want to show. This places a tick '√' character on the selected options. Selecting them again in the future, will toggle the option off.

27

Customising the Toolbar

You can customise your Toolbar from the dialogue box below which opens when you right-click on an empty section of the bar and select **C**ustomize.

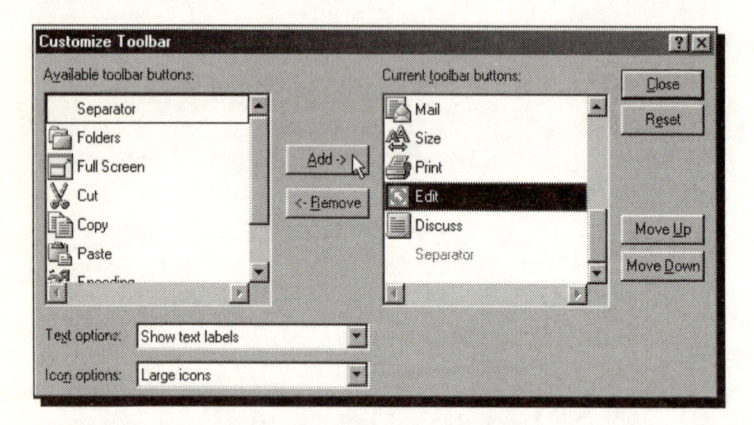

The window in the left of this box shows that there are in fact seven other Toolbar buttons available, as follows:

Folders Opens a Folders bar on the left of the Explorer window, so that you can easily access files on your computer.

Fullscreen Sets the browser to display a full screen view but leaving a customisable Toolbar for viewing control. This is a superb feature.

Cut Cuts the current selection to the clipboard.

Copy Copies the current selection to the clipboard.

Paste Pastes the clipboard contents.

Encoding Lets you change the way the browser decodes Web pages from other countries.

Related Opens the Search bar to find Web pages with a similar content to the one you are currently viewing.

Basic Program Features 3

To add any of these new buttons to the Toolbar, simply select them in the **Available toolbar buttons** list and click the central **Add** button. To remove unwanted buttons from the bar you do the reverse and select them in the **Current toolbar buttons** list and then click on **Remove**. At any time, you can click the **Reset** button to return to the default Toolbar configuration.

If, like us, you find the Toolbar buttons a little on the large side you can change the way they appear on your screen. You have three choices in the **Text options** drop-down list, and once you are used to the program, selecting the **No text labels** option removes the text completely and brings the icons much closer together.

We go one step further by selecting **Small icons** in the **Icon options** drop-down list. It is worthwhile experimenting with the settings here to find out which way you prefer your browser to operate.

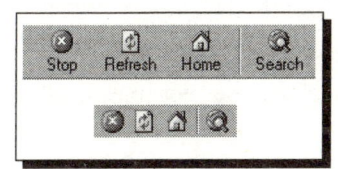

Our example here shows the difference in the size of icons after these operations have been carried out. The 'before' and 'after' sections of the Toolbar are both displayed at the same scale.

With Explorer 5, you can also alter the layout of the Control bars by dragging the bars up or down with the mouse pointer, as shown in the sequence below. The control area shrinks as you drag the frame up and expands again when it is dragged down.

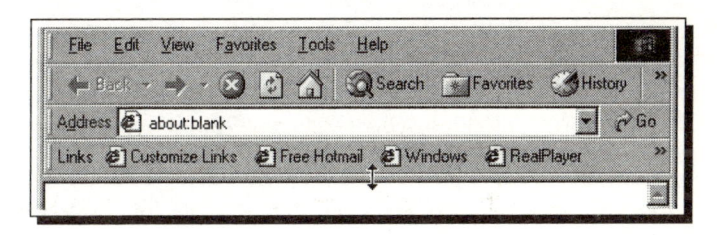

29

3   Basic Program Features

You can also try different combinations of controls in the same bars by dragging the vertical embossed lines between them. We show below our favourite arrangement of the control area, which includes all the important features, but takes up the minimum of screen space.

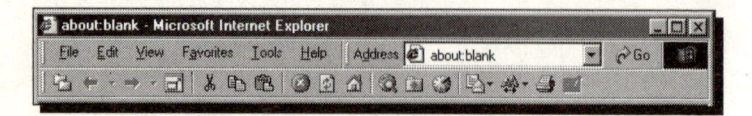

The Address Bar

The **Address** bar is the main way of opening new Web pages. If you know the URL address of the page you want to look at, you can type it into this field. Then simply clicking the **Go** button, or pressing the <Enter> key will load the page, as long as you are connected. If you are not, it will start the connection procedure. A pull-down menu, opened by clicking the down-arrow at the right of the field, lets you choose from the most recent locations you have entered, which can save some typing!

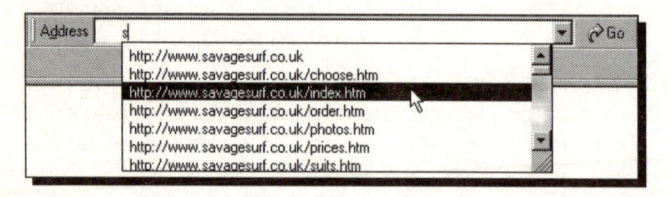

The address bar also uses 'Autocomplete' a new and very useful feature. As you start to type a URL into the address bar, Explorer drops down a list of possible matches, as shown above. As you can see, you don't usually need to type the http://www part of the address. If you have previously visited the site, you get a scrolling list of all the matching pages visited. You press the Return key to accept the default suggestion, pick the one you want from the list, or just keep typing if the address you want is not shown.

Basic Program Features

The address bar also automatically corrects common mistakes made in the 'http://' and 'ftp://' part of an address.

You can also carry out an 'Auto-Search' from the address bar, by typing '?' or 'Go' and then the words you want to search for. When you press the Return key the search will be performed. You can turn off this feature, and adjust some of the other search features in the **Advanced** tab sheet of the **Tools**, **Internet Options** dialogue box, as shown below.

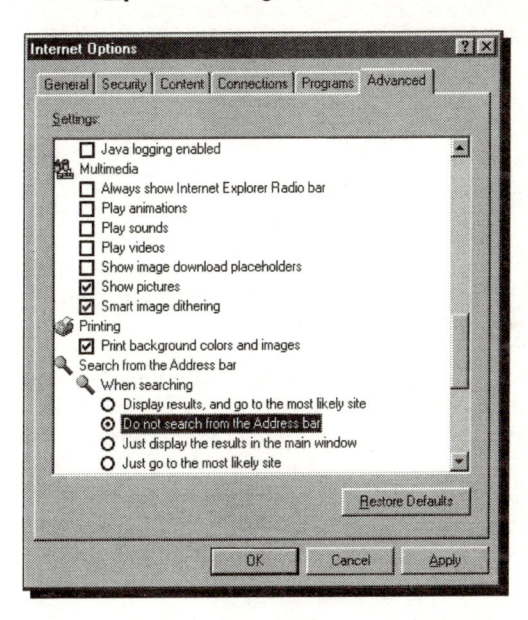

While this box is open it is worth seeing what control you do have over the browser settings. In our example above, for example, we have 'turned off' the options to play animations, sounds and videos. This was done by simply clicking in the square box to the left of each item. Clicking again will turn the option back on and place a tick in the box.

Turning off the above options will considerably speed up the loading of many Web pages. You could even go one step further and de-select the **Show pictures** option. This will turbo-charge the browser, but make the Web a little boring, unless, of course, it is only the text you are interested in.

31

The Links Bar

As we saw earlier in the chapter, by default, under the Address bar there is a set of Links buttons which open various online pages prepared for you by Microsoft, or the Internet Service Provider who supplied your browser. These links are well worth exploring and may give you some ideas about where to go on the Web, and indeed, what can be usefully achieved instead of just surfing aimlessly from one link to another.

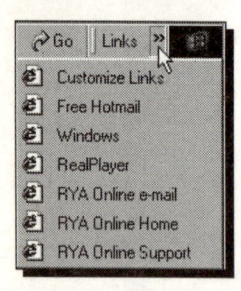

To make more room for viewing Web pages we usually turn off this feature, but a useful trick is to drag the Links bar to the right of another bar and shrink it so that all the link buttons disappear. You can then click the right arrow button to open a menu with all the links of the bar available, as shown here.

The Links buttons do not have to stay pointing to your ISP pages as shown here. You can easily set them to hold your own most used sites, as is described in the next chapter.

Fullscreen View

A feature of Explorer 5 is the option to browse using a full screen view. We often view the Web with several windows open at the same time, and so that we can see them all, they obviously have to be reduced in size. When you want to look at one page in more detail, clicking the Fullscreen icon on the Toolbar, or pressing the **F11** key, shows it using the whole screen, except for a thin Toolbar along the top edge, and reduced scroll bars if necessary. Even the Toolbar can be customised by right-clicking it. With the screen resolution we use, we can get the Toolbar icons, the Menu bar and the Address bar onto the Fullscreen Toolbar. We usually have **Auto Hide** selected as well, so that the Toolbar itself only displays when you move the pointer over it.

Basic Program Features 3

The rest of the time the Web page is displayed with no Windows 'clutter' at all, as in our example below.

This option really makes viewing Web pages a pleasure. For this alone, it would be worth converting to Explorer 5! Clicking the Fullscreen icon, or pressing **F11**, again returns you to the window layout you had before.

General Option Settings

Like most Windows programs, you control the other ways Internet Explorer operates for you, by changing settings in a series of tabbed sheets accessed with the **Tools**, **Internet Options** menu command, as we saw earlier. Perhaps we should now look at some of the other options available here.

In the **General** tab sheet, shown open on the next page, you can control which page is loaded when you start Explorer, or click the Home icon. We are sure you will not want the Microsoft default **Home page** option, so we suggest you load the page you do want before you open this dialogue box and then select the **Use Current** option.

3 Basic Program Features

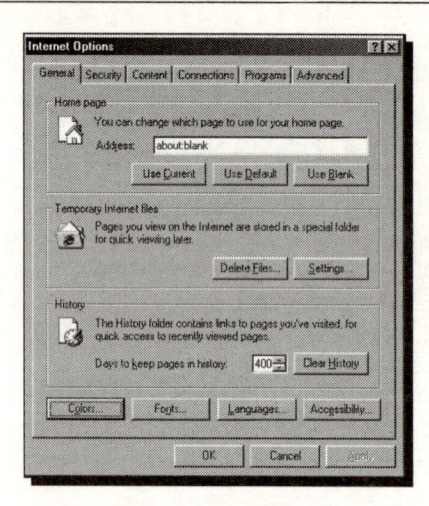

The **Temporary Internet files** options let you control the hard disc cache where the program stores all the files it downloads. The **History** section gives you some control over the details of the pages you have recently visited which are displayed when you click the History Toolbar icon. If you ever run short of hard disc space, clearing these two options will release that space being used for temporary file storage.

The **Fonts** and **Languages** buttons let you set the default fonts and language used by your browser, and the **Accessibility** button lets you override any font size, colour or type settings made in a Web page. This is not usually a good thing to do, unless you have very strong preferences, as Web page authors usually spend a lot of time specifying their page settings to get the visual effects they want.

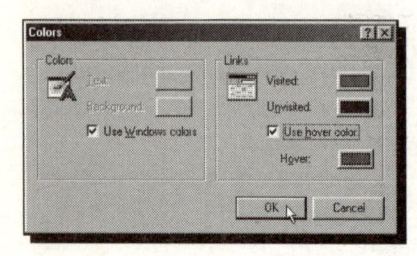

The **Colors** button gives you control of the colours in a Web page. We suggest you leave the **Use Windows colors** option selected, but select **Use hover color** as shown here.

Basic Program Features 3

With 'hover' colour set, as shown, the links on a Web page change colour to a bright red whenever you pass the pointer over them.

While you are at it, take a good look around the other options on the other tabbed sheets. If an option is not self explanatory, you can click the help button shown here (which is located in the top right of the window), then click the 'What's this' pointer on the offending item to get more details of its function, as shown below.

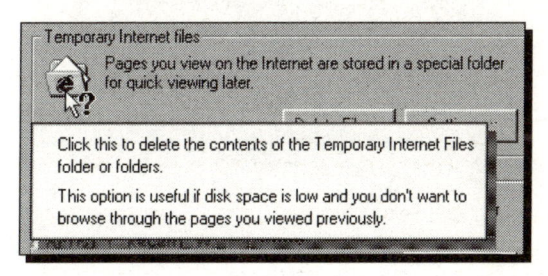

Saving Pictures

For many people, one of the big attractions of the Internet is the enormous collection of photographs and other graphical data that is freely available. Whatever your preferences, all you have to do is search until you find what you are looking for.

But how can I download a picture onto my PC and have it to look at, whenever I want? I hear you asking.

If you have followed this chapter up to this point you will not need to ask, you will probably be doing it already. If not, the procedure is very easy. Once you have found the picture you want on a Web page, simply right-click your mouse on it and select from the object menu that opens.

Our example on the next page shows a photograph from one of our Web sites of a consultant surveying, with the right-click menu options that are available. Clicking on **Save Picture As...** will open the Save As dialogue box for you to

3 Basic Program Features

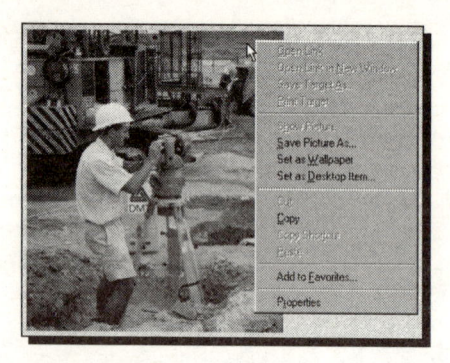

enter the **File name** and folder to **Save in** details. When you have done this, simply click the **Save** button to capture your picture. Don't fill up your hard disc though!

Explorer Help

The trend these days is for programs to be shipped with very little in the way of a manual and a much less detailed built-in Help system than was the norm a few years ago. We shouldn't really complain about this as maybe that is why you are reading this book!

Internet Explorer 5 has a built-in Help system, which is accessed with the **Help**, **Contents and Index** menu command, or the **F1** keystroke. This opens a Windows 98 type Help window, as shown on the next page.

We strongly recommend that you work your way through all the listed items. Clicking on a closed book icon will open it and display a listing of its contents. Double-clicking on a list item will open a window with a few lines of Help information.

Another way of browsing the Help system is to click the **Index** tab and work your way through the alphabetic listing. The **Favourites** tab is a new feature which opens a page that lets you store help screens that you may want to refer to again.

Basic Program Features

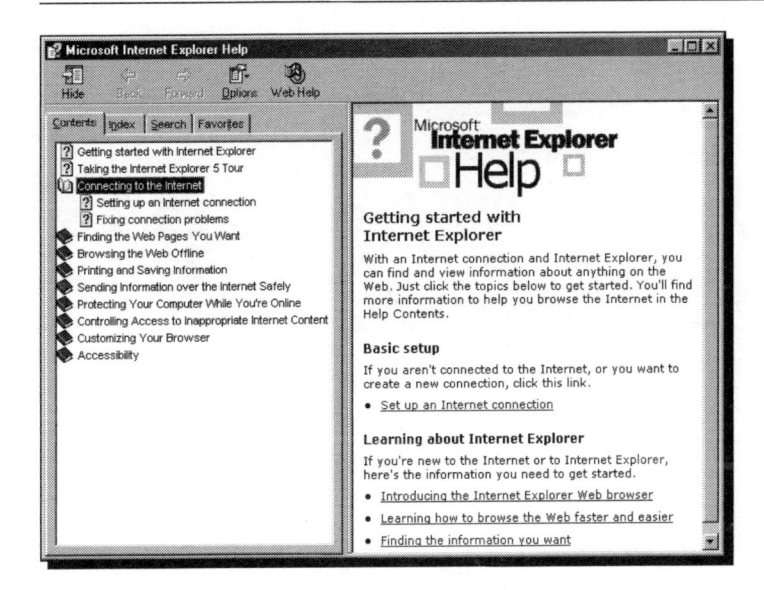

The **Search** tab opens a search facility you can use, as shown below. In this example we typed 'saving pictures' in the **Type in the keyword to find** text field and clicked the **List Topics** button. Then, selecting the one **Topic** found and clicking **Display**, opened Help information on it.

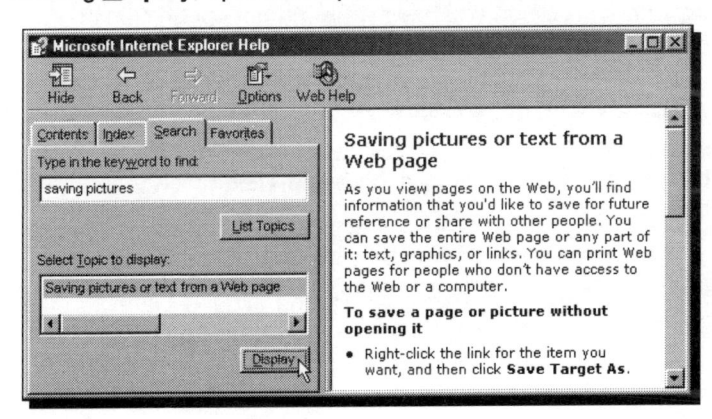

The Help provided by Microsoft with version 5 of the browser leaves much to be desired, but there is also more help available from their Web site.

37

3 Basic Program Features

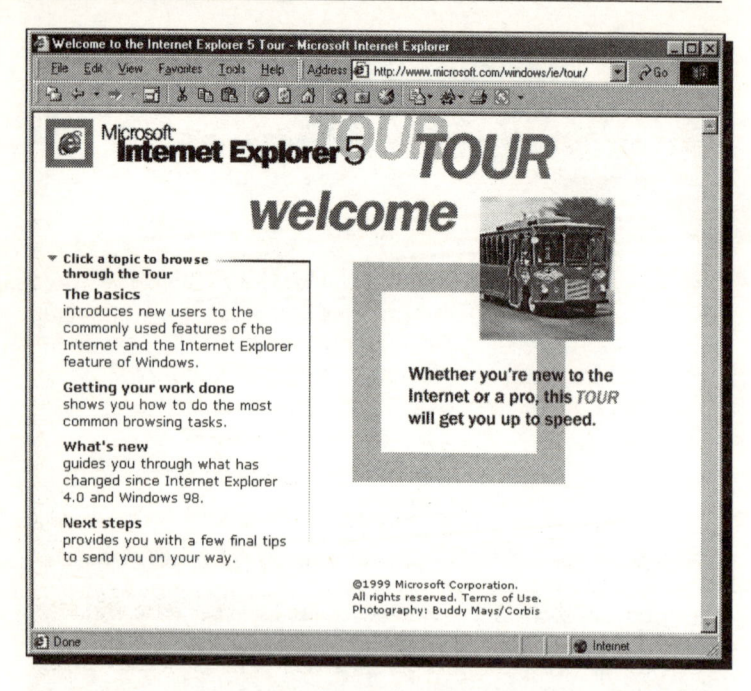

To get the 'live' tutorial shown above, use the **Help**, **Tour** menu commands and just follow the links. This, of course, will only work when you have your Internet connection open!

Another Online Tutorial

Another basic on-line Web tutorial provided by Microsoft, can be accessed by typing the following URL into the Address Bar.

> http://www.microsoft.com/insider/internet

If you are new to it, this may well be a good place to start your Web browsing, but it can be a little slow at times, depending on the amount of traffic crossing the Atlantic.

4

More Skills and Features

As we saw in the last chapter, either your ISP or Microsoft will have provided a starting page for your Web browsing. These are, as you would expect, really professional pages with point and click links to other pages of interest. Most you can even customise to show the type of information you are interested in, and then make it your home page.

You can also see in our screen dump above, an example of the advertising that is now a feature on many Web pages. The search engine pages also seem to be getting weighed down with it. Generating advertising revenue certainly helps to pay for some of our 'free' Web facilities, but at the expense of speed. Every graphic has to be downloaded and takes valuable time.

A Useful Starting Site

When you get fed up with surfing between sites which offer all manner of visual and audio entertainment, you might like to visit one useful page we often revisit. Try entering the following address, which points to an American University site, so hopefully it will stay active. But don't forget things can change overnight on the Web.

http://www.ithaca.edu/Library/Training/useful.html

The header of this page is shown below. It is maintained by a librarian with a sense of humour and points to an interesting array of reference and other kinds of library oriented sites.

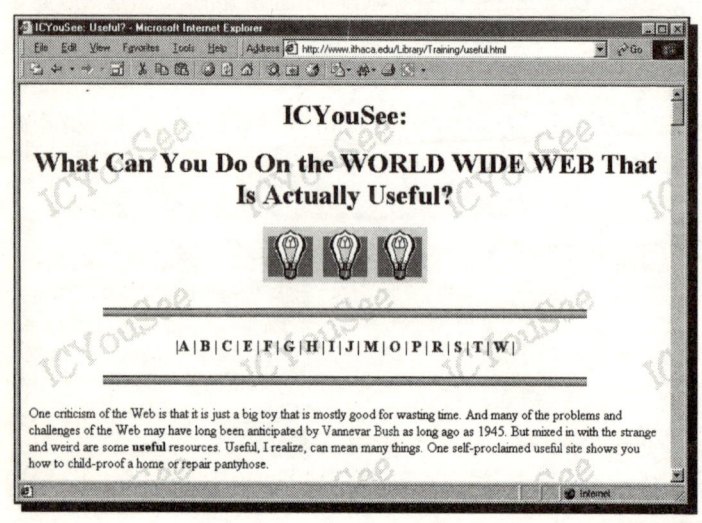

Using Web Information

Once you have found what you were looking for on the Web you can, with very little in the way of basic skills, save it to your own PC and use it for your own purposes. Most Web pages consist of HTML code, text, graphic or video images, sound files, or links to files of some sort that have been used in the page construction. All of these can be saved for your own use, as we shall see.

The Mouse Pointer

You have almost certainly noticed by now that the mouse pointer changes shape depending on what part of a page it is pointing to. There are three main shapes:

The main pointer which shows over inactive areas of a page. You cannot do anything in these areas.

The hand pointer that appears when you move over a link. Clicking the right mouse button opens a menu of actions you can carry out with that link, or its file.

The I beam pointer that means you can select the text beneath it.

Copying Text

You can copy selected, or highlighted, text from an Explorer page to the Windows clipboard with the **Edit**, **Copy** menu command, the <Ctrl+C> shortcut, or the Copy Toolbar icon (if you have placed it on the Toolbar). If you want to copy all the text on a page, it is quicker to select it with the <Ctrl+A> keyboard shortcut, or the **Edit**, **Select All** command. The copied text will have any HTML tags stripped out, with the exception of any contained hyperlinks. These will still be active if the program you paste the text into supports them

Once the text you want is on the clipboard, you can **Paste** it, <Ctrl+V>, into whatever open Windows application program you want, and then save it. Notepad is useful for this, or WordPad for a lot of text. But remember, the text might look formatted in WordPad, but this is only done with imported space characters. In either case, you will almost certainly have to do some editing to remove lots of unwanted empty spaces.

4 More Skills and Features

Viewing Source Code

If you want to see what the code for any page actually looks like, you can use the **View**, **Source** command. This opens the file in Notepad, so you can edit it as well and save it wherever you want, except back to its Web site, of course. Our example below shows some of the actual HTML source code for the Web page displayed on page 33.

```
index.html - Notepad
File Edit Search Help
<!DOCTYPE HTML PUBLIC "-//W3C//DTD HTML 3.2//EN">
<html>

<head>
<meta name="Author" content="Phil Oliver">
<meta name="Description" content="Site of Michael Strang, the contemporary British artist
and oil painter of seascapes, landscapes, portraits and flowers. An exhibition of over 200
drawings and paintings, with some art for sale and a limited edition print issue.">
<meta name="GENERATOR" content="Microsoft FrontPage 4.0">
<meta name="KeyWords" content="Surrey, Cornwall, English artist, artist, landscape artist,
landscape, dandelions, seascape, Michael Strang, picture, oil painting, prints for sale,
Cornwall, Cornish artist, painter, English, British, limited edition print, portrait,
poppy, poppies, Penzance, Gulval, contemporary art, exhibition, gallery, galleries, flowers,
sunflowers, cornfield, Royal Academy, Tate, still life, commissions, St Ives, Porthmeor
beach, canvas, museum, contemporary, still life">
<meta name="ProgId" content="FrontPage.Editor.Document">
<title>Michael Strang - British artist - landscapes, seascapes, portraits and
flowers</title>

<script language="javascript">
function GotoURL(f) {
        top.location.href = f.picker.options[f.picker.selectedIndex].value;
        }
</script>

</head>

<body text="#000000" bgcolor="#FFFFFF" link="#0000EE" vlink="#551A8B" alink="#FF0000"
background="background.gif">
```

Saving a Target Link

Explorer has a way of saving a Web file without you even having to open it. If you right-click your mouse pointer on a link in an open page, an object menu is opened, as we have seen before.

Selecting the **Save Target As** option from this menu, and completing the details of file name and destination folder in the **Save As** box, will start the download process. While this download is taking place a message window is opened with a progress bar that indicates how the process is proceeding, and shows an estimate of the remaining time that will be taken.

More Skills and Features 4

Saving Whole Pages

There are several reasons for wanting to save a whole Web page to your own disc drive:

So that you can edit the source code to form the basis of a page of your own. Don't forget copyrights.

To create a hypertext 'reference book' of pages you have down-loaded. This would then work on any PC that had the files on it. Web based tutorials, maybe.

To use embedded links in a file as instant Bookmarks.

Before version 5 of Explorer, you could not easily save whole Web pages, including their pictures, etc., to your hard disc. That has now changed, and you now have several options available from the Save Web Page box shown below, which is opened with the **File**, **Save As** menu command.

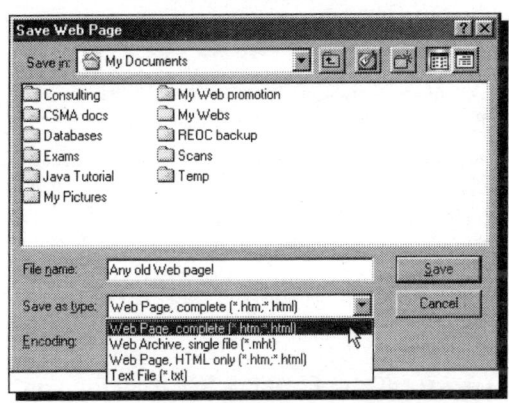

As shown there are four choices in the **Save as type** box, the first two being new to this version of Internet Explorer.

Web Page, Complete (*.htm, *.html)

This is the most useful one which allows you to save the page to a folder on your hard drive. It will save the HTML page as one file, and all the graphics, audio and other contained files as other linked files on your disc. The links

43

and references within the HTML page will be adjusted so as to refer to the new local locations of all the contained files saved on your hard drive.

You can then open the standard HTML file on your drive and the full page, with all graphics and extras will be loaded without requiring connection to the Internet.

Web Archive, Single File (*.mht)

This option is available if you have installed Outlook Express 5 and lets you save an offline version of a Web page and all its contained graphics as a single archive '.mht' file. At the moment it seems that this file format is only used by Explorer 5 and Outlook Express 5, but it is useful if you want to send the page by e-mail. But remember that the recipient must also be using Internet Explorer 5 and Outlook Express 5. Unfortunately page backgrounds seem to get lost with this process.

Web Page, HTML Only (*.htm, *.html)

This is the option that was available previously, which lets you save the current Explorer page with all the HTML codes still in place. A page saved in this way does not retain its graphics, only the text and codes. If you want to use the page again with your browser, but are not worried about the contained graphics, then save it this way.

Text File (*.txt)

This simply allows you to save the text from the page with all the HTML code stripped out. You might use this method to save the text of a whole Web page that you wanted to include in a word processor document.

More Skills and Features 4

Downloading a Program File

If you capture many graphics you may well need a program to quickly view and manipulate them. A good shareware program we have come across to do this is LView Pro, and as an example we will step you through the process of downloading this from the Internet.

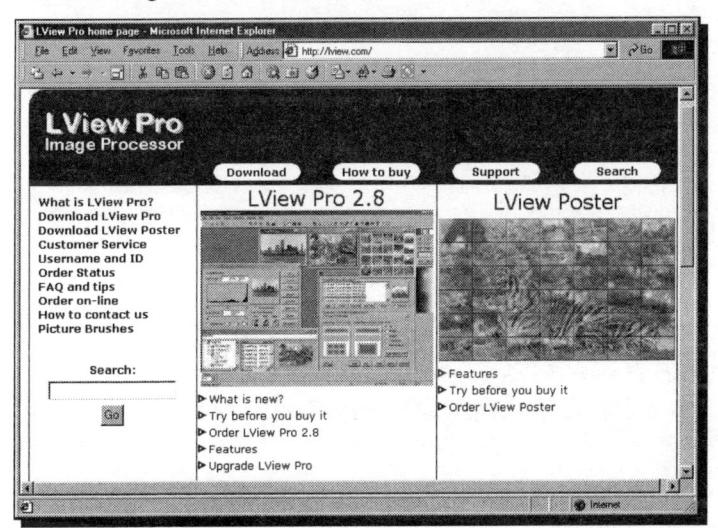

To open the home page, shown above, type the following URL in the Address bar and press <Enter>:

http://www.lview.com

Clicking the **Download** button link opens a page with some details of how to download the program.

> DOWNLOAD LView Pro 2.8
> After download is complete, use the Windows Explorer to check if the file size is 1,966,134 bytes (1,921 KB or 1.87 MB). If not, try to download it again.

If you want, you can action the **DOWNLOAD...** link shown above to start the process, which is in fact an FTP operation.

The warning box shown next is opened to make you aware that there is a danger of importing viruses if you download

45

4 More Skills and Features

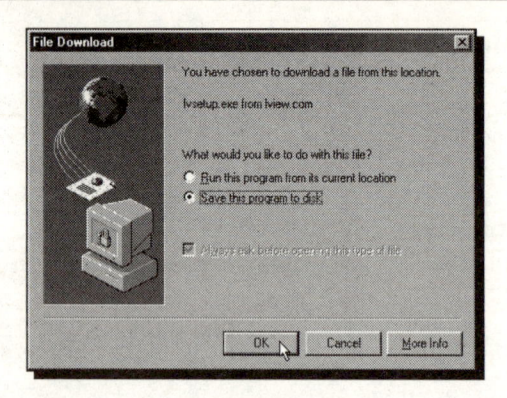

program files from an unknown source. The provider of this program should be a safe source, so make sure the **Save this program to disk** option is selected and click the **OK** button.

Complete the details in the **Save As** dialogue box, (we suggest you save it to a temporary folder called **Temp**), and click **Save** to start downloading. This opens the File Download box as shown here, and as long as this box is open the downloading is still taking place. With a modem connection, this process took us over ten minutes.

In our case above, a flurry of disc activity and the closing of the message box indicates the completion of the operation. If you leave the **Close this dialog box when download completes** option unchecked, the options to **Open** the downloaded file and **Open Folder** are activated when the operation is finished.

More Skills and Features

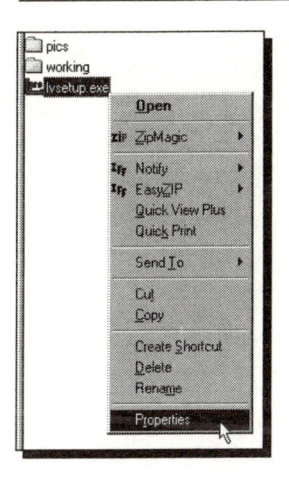

We suggest you click the **Open Folder** button to check that the file has been received on your system. This should open the **Temp** folder in a 'My Computer' window, and you should see it there as shown in our example on the left.

If you want to find out more about the file you could right-click the mouse pointer on its icon and select the **Properties** option from the opened menu. This opens a tabbed dialogue box giving two pages of details about the file.

Once you have followed the online instructions and installed LView Pro you will have a very useful graphic utility program to evaluate. Of course, as it is shareware, if you carry on using it you will have to pay a registration fee.

An Internet Software Source

A favourite site of ours for finding extra Internet and other software is run by the TUCOWS Network, and it is well worth taking a look at one of their sites. If you are thinking of downloading anything from the Internet you should try and find the nearest site to you that you can so as to save on downloading time. Tucows (sorry about the name) have a mirror site at the following address:

http://www.mirror.ac.uk/sites/ftp.tucows.com/tucows

A few minutes looking around this site is well worth anybody's time. You can find some very powerful and free programs to download and try out.

Printing Web Pages

It was originally thought by some, that computers would lead to the paperless office. That has certainly not proved to be correct. It seems that however good our electronic communication media becomes most people want to see the results printed on paper. As far as books are concerned, long may that last!

Microsoft have built into Explorer 5 the ability to produce the best printed output of Web pages we have so far seen. There is now a preview option, pages with frames are handled and you can also control the headers and footers that are printed. The screen layout of most Web pages with a text content depends on the size of the window you have open and the font size you are using. Try this out by viewing a text-based page full screen and then reducing it to a smaller window. The page will be reformatted around any embedded graphics. The same thing happens when you print, except that the paper size, not the window, determines the eventual layout.

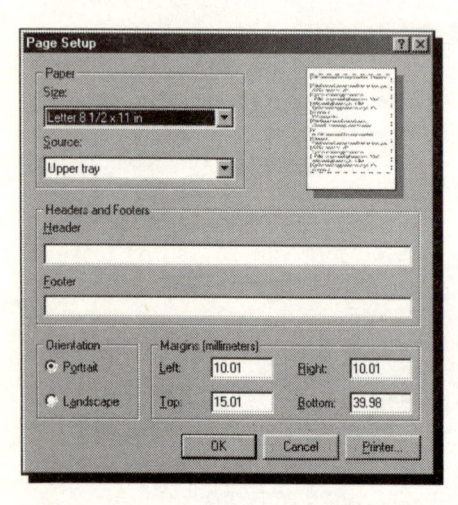

Before you print, you should check the page settings with the **File**, **Page Setup** command, which opens the dialogue box shown here. The usual options of paper **Size** and **Source**, **Margins** and **Orientation** are controlled here, as well as those of **Header** and **Footer**. The Help section, shown on the next page is perhaps the easiest way to come to terms with how to control these two features.

More Skills and Features 4

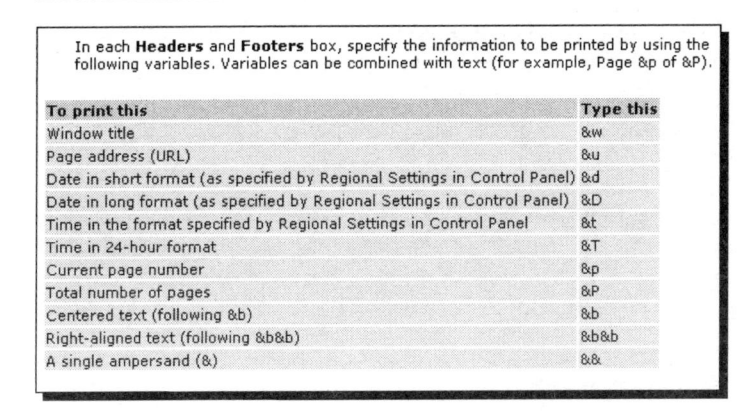

In each **Headers** and **Footers** box, specify the information to be printed by using the following variables. Variables can be combined with text (for example, Page &p of &P).

To print this	Type this
Window title	&w
Page address (URL)	&u
Date in short format (as specified by Regional Settings in Control Panel)	&d
Date in long format (as specified by Regional Settings in Control Panel)	&D
Time in the format specified by Regional Settings in Control Panel	&t
Time in 24-hour format	&T
Current page number	&p
Total number of pages	&P
Centered text (following &b)	&b
Right-aligned text (following &b&b)	&b&b
A single ampersand (&)	&&

When you are ready to print, use the <Ctrl+P> key combination, or the **File**, **Print** menu command, to open the Print dialogue box shown below. If you use the Print Toolbar button this box does not open and the last settings are used.

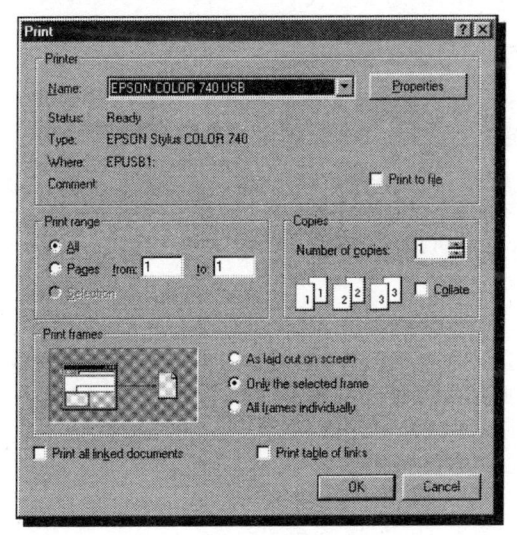

Make sure the correct printer is selected, choose the pages to be printed, how many copies you want, how you want any page frames to print, and finally click **OK** to start the printing process. You should be impressed with the results, we certainly were.

49

4 More Skills and Features

There are two very useful features in the above dialogue box, that we have not yet seen elsewhere:

- The **Print table of links** option, which when checked, gives a hard copy listing of the URL addresses of all the links present in the printed Web page.

- The **Print all linked documents** option, which not only prints the current Web page, but all those linked to it. This is a great way to print a whole Web site, as long as its links are not too deeply embedded.

Print Preview

A new feature added to later versions of Explorer 5 allows you to preview your print output on screen. About time too! If you use this before printing you can get a good idea if it is worth attempting to print the page. As you may have found out, some Web pages just will not print properly. The results of using the **File**, **Print Preview** command with one of our Web pages are shown below.

The toolbar lets you move between pages, zoom them in and out, open the Page Setup box and finally, when you are happy, lets you send the page to your printer.

History Files

Explorer stores all the Web pages and files you view on your hard disc, and places temporary pointers to them all in the **Windows/History** folder. To return to them in the future, first use the **File**, **Work Offline** command and then click the History icon on the Toolbar which opens the History Explorer bar, as shown below. In this vertical bar, you can scroll offline through the sites you have recently visited. Moving the pointer over the entries will open a banner giving details of the dates, or file locations involved. Clicking on a blue 'date' icon opens a list of the sites visited. Clicking on a site will open a list of the pages you accessed there, and selecting one of these will open it for you.

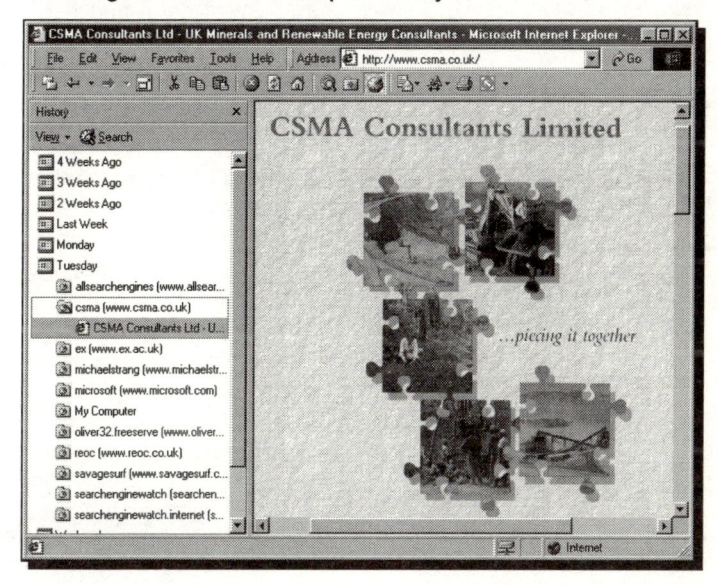

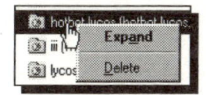

Right-clicking on any list item gives you the options to **Expand** (or open) it, or to **Delete** it, as shown here.

4   More Skills and Features

This gives you the option of editing out any pages you don't want.

You can control the length of time that Explorer keeps this History information in the settings sheet that is opened with the **Tools**, **Internet Options**, command.

Ours was set for 400 days, as shown above, so all the saved History files expire 400 days after they are last visited. Whether our hard disc will cope with this amount of data remains to be seen. You can delete them all immediately by clicking the **Clear History** button, to release the hard disc space used.

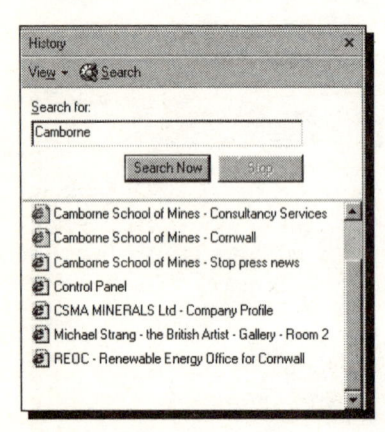

You can now search through the files in your History list for a specific word or phrase, by clicking the **Search** button, typing the text wanted and finally clicking the **Search Now** button. An example of a single word search is shown above. All the pages stored in the History that contain the text searched for are listed.

The **View** button, as shown here, gives you four ways of ranking the list in the History bar.

52

More Skills and Features

The Cache

You may have noticed that a Web page, especially one with lots of graphics, loads more quickly into Explorer if you have already recently viewed it. This is because all the pages and files you view are stored in a cache on your hard disc, which is in fact a system folder called 'Temporary Internet files', located in the Windows folder. The next time you access that page, depending on your settings, Explorer checks to see if the page has been updated before bringing it from the cache. If any change to the page has occurred, the new version is downloaded. If not, a cached copy is quickly retrieved. As with the History files, you control the cache, from the Options box which is opened with the **Tools**, **Internet Options** command.

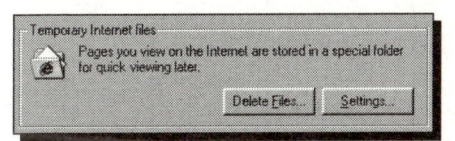

The Temporary Internet files section of the General settings tabbed sheet is shown above. Pressing the **Delete Files** button will clear the cache, which will very rapidly free up space on your hard disc. The **Settings** button will open the following control box.

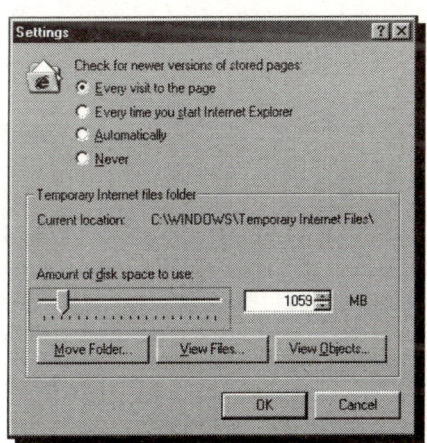

This shows that, in our case, these temporary files are stored in a cache in the C:\Windows\Temporary Internet Files folder, and that Web sites are checked for changes **Every visit to the page**. To guarantee that you always view the most up to date version of Web pages this is a good setting, but page loading may be a little slower. You can also press the Refresh icon, or the **F5** key to refresh the current page being viewed. If there is a newer version of the page on its server this will then be downloaded to your PC. This does not always work properly with 'framed' pages though.

If you are short of space on your hard disc, you can reduce the size of your cache by lowering the **Amount of disk space to use** slider. Again this will reduce the number of sites that can be cached, and may slow you down. If you have another hard disc you could also move the cache onto it by clicking the **Move Folder** button. The **View Files** option lets you look in the cache, and the **View Objects** button lets you look in the Downloaded Programs folder, but the only operations you can perform in these folders are to open and view the contained files; even that option has a warning message, and is not recommended.

Any operations you carry out on the files in your cache, such as moving or deleting them, may affect any settings you have activated in the **Favorites** sub-menu, as described in a later chapter.

Security

Because of its design, the Internet itself does not provide security for any data transmitted across it. As we saw in Chapter 1, data travelling between your computer and a server somewhere else in the world passes through a large number of computer systems. An operator at any one of these computers has the potential to view, manipulate, or even corrupt, your data, which can thus be very susceptible to fraud or other misuse by unscrupulous individuals.

For most casual Web browsing this would not really matter, but if you are conducting business, or sending sensitive personal information, such as details of your credit card, you need security measures to make sure that your data is safe.

Explorer Security Measures

Netscape Communications originally developed a security technology called SSL, (short for Secure Sockets Layer protocol), which has become a standard since it was put into the public domain for the Internet community. This SSL protocol checks the identity of the server being accessed, carries out data encryption of any messages sent, and guarantees their general integrity. SSL is layered beneath the Internet application protocols (HTTP, Telnet, FTP, Gopher, etc.), but above the TCP/IP connection protocol. In this way it operates independently of the Internet protocols.

Microsoft Explorer supports SSL, as well as PCT (Private Communication Technology), which enables you to make secure credit-card purchases from a Web page. With these active on both your browser and the server you are transmitting to, your sensitive communications should be absolutely secure and unusable by third parties.

With Explorer you can tell whether a page or document comes from a secure server by looking at the status bar. If a padlock icon is placed there when the page is opened, the site is secure.

Security Zones

To help protect your computer from downloading or running possibly harmful files, Explorer 5 divides your browsing world into zones, and allows you to assign sites to a zone with a suitable security level. You can tell which zone a current Web page is in by looking at the right side of the status bar, as shown here. Whenever you attempt to open or download content from the Web, Explorer checks the security settings for that Web site's zone. There are four zones and by default, pages downloaded from a Web site are given the medium security settings associated

4 More Skills and Features

with the **Internet zone**. Double-clicking on the Security rating on the status bar opens the box shown below.

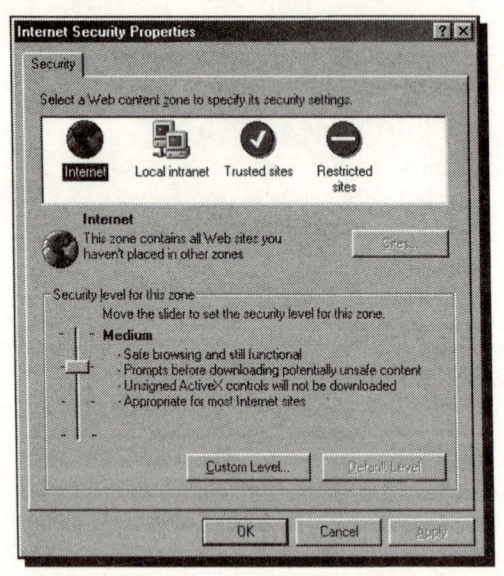

This Security settings sheet is also opened with the **Tools**, **Internet Options** command. If you are worried about your system being 'contaminated' from a Web site, click the **Sites** button here and give the site a **Restricted sites** rating.

A Secure Transaction

As an example of a typical secure transaction carried out with Explorer 5, we will step through the process of ordering our copy of the shareware program LView Pro which we downloaded earlier in the chapter.

From the LView Pro home page, shown on page 45, clicking the link shown here, eventually opens a Security Alert box which warns you that you are about to enter a secure page.

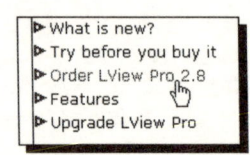

- What is new?
- Try before you buy it
- Order LView Pro 2.8
- Features
- Upgrade LView Pro

More Skills and Features 4

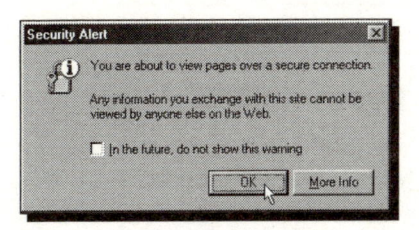

You have the options to disable this warning for the future, to get **More Info,** or to click **OK** to continue.

The above part page shows the padlock icon displayed in the status bar, indicating the Web page is secure. When you move the pointer over the padlock icon the level of site security is flagged as also shown above. By right-clicking the icon you can open a copy of the actual security certificate properties. You can also tell that the page is secure, by looking at the start of its URL in the Address bar; if it begins with 'https:' instead of 'http:', it is a secure page.

New Explorer Components

We saw in Chapter 2 that when Explorer 5 is installed on your PC a typical set of components is usually put there. These may work well for a long time, but eventually you will encounter a Web page that requires an Explorer component that you don't have. With us the following box opened a few weeks ago.

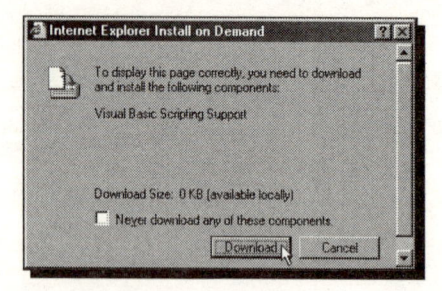

We needed the Visual Basic Scripting Support component, but Explorer was offering to automatically download it for us. All we had to do was click the **Download** button, and a few minutes later all was well. This 'Install on Demand' feature really is excellent.

5

Where Shall We Go Today?

For anyone not involved with the Web, Microsoft's recent advertising catch phrase "Where do you want to go today?" was probably a bit confusing. For those that do a little surfing the confusion must be, how do we choose where to go?

You can literally spend hours following links from one place to another, and at the end of the day sometimes getting nowhere useful. But if you want some specific information you will have to use one, or more, of the many search tools, or 'engines' that are available.

The Search Assistant

We introduced the Search button and bar earlier on page 26, when we did an initial search. What we used then was actually the new Search Assistant, as shown here.

When you open the Search bar, you now have a selection of types of searches you can perform.

Find a Web Page - Looks for specific web pages containing the searched-for information. Only three search engines were available to us, Excite, UK Plus and MSN Web Search.

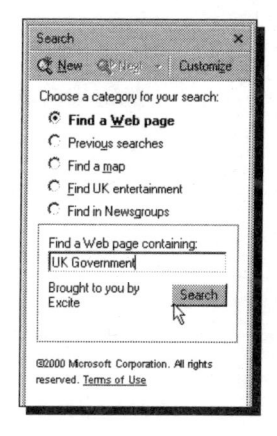

59

5 Where Shall We Go Today?

Previous searches - Locates information in the last ten searches you carried out. It displays the searches as a list of hyperlinks that you can follow to the returned search results.

Find a map - Searches for a place or address and tries to find a map for you. Only expedia.com was available to us, which was not one of the better map sites for the UK!

Find a word - Looks up an entered word in either the Encarta Encyclopaedia, a dictionary or a thesaurus.

Find in newsgroups - uses Dejanews to locate specific information from newsgroup postings. We cover the newsgroups in a later chapter.

To use any of these, you select it from the list and complete the 'question boxes' that are opened. The idea is very good, but the search tools offered in most of the options are very limited and in some cases only of major use in the US.

Customising the Assistant

If you click the **Customize** button a new window opens in which you can, to some extent, control how the Assistant works.

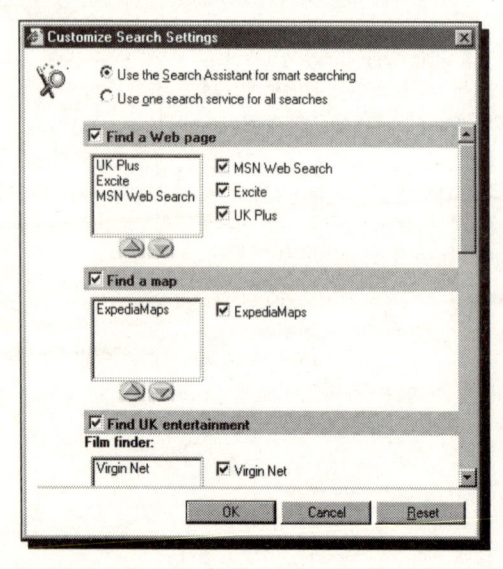

You can only use the search engines that are available in the lists above. Hopefully they will be added to over time. Parts of this window are also a little confusing, such as 'Find UK Entertainment' which does not actually appear in the Assistant list. The idea seems to be that you can select which engines are used for each type of search, and rank them as well. An excellent idea but not carried through to the end user. Perhaps we should say, "watch this space!" and also keep our fingers crossed.

Search Tools

There are a number of search tools, or engines, available to help you find what you want on the Web. Some search all the contents of documents, others only the file name. Most of them rank the search results in order depending on the number of times the searched-for words appear in a document, or on some other criteria.

Basically there are two types:

- Directories, like Yahoo, depend on people to submit a short description to the directory with the URL for new sites, which are then reviewed. A search request to the directory then looks for matches only in the descriptions submitted.

- Search engines like AltaVista, Lycos and Infoseek will find individual pages of a Web site that match your search, even if the site itself has nothing to do with what you are looking for.

Each search tool seems to use a different method of searching, so your search results may vary when you use different ones. Be patient as you may not always find what you're looking for very easily.

What is Available

In the next few pages we alphabetically list some of the main search tools that are available to you, with their URL addresses and a few comments on each. To access these you should type their URL into the Address bar and then hit the **Go** button. You may find it useful to build up a list of search addresses as Favorites. The next chapter will show you how.

Be patient with the search tools, they are all different. With most you simply type in the text you want to search for, but they usually offer much more complicated searches as well. If you have problems, look for a Help link and spend a few minutes reading how best to use the site's facilities. Don't forget that these are changing all the time, and no Web listing can ever be fully current!

AOL Search

http://search.aol.com

AOL Search (America On Line) allows its members to search across the web and in AOL's own content. Anyone can use the address listed above, but it does not list AOL content. Launched in October 1999.

AltaVista

http://www.altavista.com
http://www.altavista.co.uk

One of the largest search engines on the web, in terms of pages indexed. AltaVista opened in December 1995 and is one of our favourites. They recently announced their plan to provide free phone access to the Internet in the UK.

Ask Jeeves

http://www.askjeeves.com

A human-powered search service that aims to direct you to the exact page that answers your question. If it fails to find a match within its own database, then it will provide matching web pages from various search engines. Opened fully on June 1, 1997. Results from Ask Jeeves also appear within AltaVista.

Where Shall We Go Today?

Deja.com
http://www.deja.com/usenet

A specialist tool that searches Usenet newsgroups, and cuts through the millions of postings with absolute ease.

Excite
http://www.excite.com

http://www.excite.co.uk

Another of the most popular search services on the Web, which offers a medium-sized index and integrates non-web material such as company information and sports scores into its results. Launched in late 1995.

FAST Search
http://www.alltheweb.com

With the ambition to index the entire Web, FAST Search launched in May 1999 and includes well over 200 million pages.

Go / Infoseek
http://www.go.com

Go is a portal site produced by Infoseek and Disney and consistently provides quality results in response to many general and broad searches, due to its ESP search algorithm. Officially launched in January 1999.

GoTo
http://www.goto.com

Unlike the other major search engines, GoTo charges companies to be ranked higher in the search results. Non-paid results come from Inktomi.

Google
http://www.google.com

This search engine makes heavy use of link popularity as a primary way to rank web sites. The more links on the Web to a site, the higher will be its ranking in a search list.

HotBot
http://www.hotbot.com

Another popular engine due to its large index of the Web. Owned by Lycos but run as a separate search service.

Inktomi
http://www.inktomi.com

The Inktomi index powers several other search services. There is no way to query the Inktomi index directly.

LookSmart
http://www.looksmart.com

A human-compiled directory of web sites. As well as being a stand-alone service, LookSmart provides directory results to MSN Search, Excite and other partners. AltaVista provides it with search engine results when a search fails to find a match from among LookSmart's reviews.

Lycos
http://www.lycos.com
http://www.lycos.co.uk

In April 1999 Lycos changed to a directory model similar to Yahoo. Its main listings come from the Open Directory project, and secondary results come from its own 'spidering' of the web.

MSN Search
http://search.msn.com

Microsoft's MSN Search service is a LookSmart-powered directory of Web sites, with secondary results from AltaVista.

Netscape Search
http://search.netscape.com

Netscape Search's results come primarily from the Open Directory and Netscape's own Smart Browsing database. Secondary results come from Google. At the Netscape Netcenter portal site, other search engines are also featured.

Northern Light
http://www.northernlight.com

Features one of the largest indexes of the Web, along with the ability to cluster documents by topic. Opened to general use in August 1997.

Open Directory
http://dmoz.org

The Open Directory uses volunteer editors to catalogue the Web. It was launched in June 1998 and acquired by Netscape that November. Lycos and AOL Search make use of Open Directory data, while AltaVista and HotBot prominently feature Open Directory categories within their results pages.

SearchUK
http://www.searchuk.com
Automatically indexes UK related domains (.co.uk etc.) and will include UK sites outside these domains (.com etc.) as long as strong UK content is notified to them.

Snap
http://www.snap.com
A human-compiled directory of Web sites, supplemented by search results from Inktomi. Launched in late 1997 and is backed by Cnet and NBC.

UK Plus
http://www.ukplus.co.uk
Features searchable reviews of UK sites, prepared by a team of journalists. Users can also perform a general search across the entire Web with Infoseek. UKPlus is owned by Associated Newspapers and launched in Jan 1997.

UKMax
http://www.ukmax.com
Powered by Inktomi, UKMax allows users to search only pages within the .uk domain or perform a worldwide search. It also offers some directory listings, regional news content, weather reports, and portal features such as portfolio tracking.

WebCrawler
http://www.webcrawler.com
Has the smallest index of any major search engine on the Web. Owned by Excite but run as an independent search engine.

Yahoo
http://www.yahoo.com
Probably the most popular search service and is the largest human-compiled guide to the Web, employing about 150 editors. Yahoo has well over 1 million sites listed and supplements its directory results with those from Inktomi.

Deja.com - As an Example

We cannot include examples of all the search tools listed, but to give you an idea of their power we have dabbled with a Deja search. For anyone starting to get to grips with the Usenet newsgroups this tool is essential. As we saw earlier, the address of the Deja site is:

http://www.deja.com/usenet

This opens the Web page shown below. Unfortunately the whole site has been redesigned and much of it now looks like all the other portals. Some of its facilities have either been lost, or hidden too deep in the site for us to find. Progress?

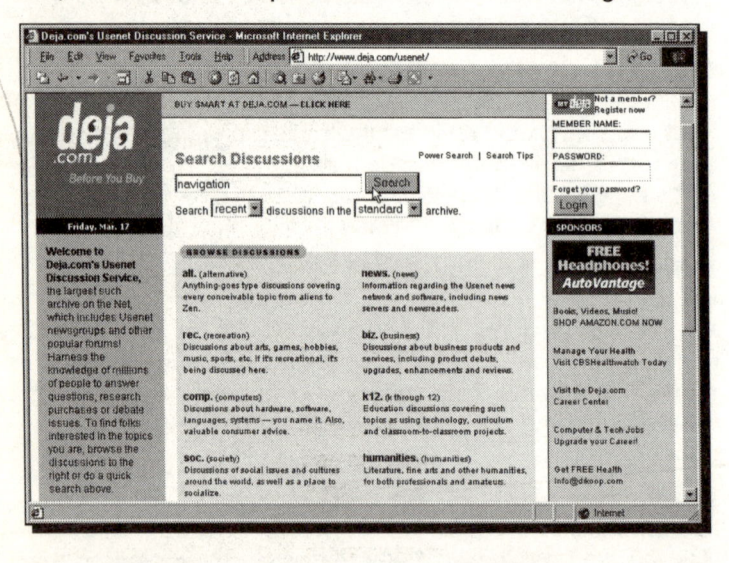

You can browse the discussion (or Usenet) groups, or search them which is what we will do. We are interested in sailing and generally finding our way around the oceans, so we entered **navigation** in the **Search** box and then pressed the **Search** button. The first few of the 7,432 search results are shown on the next page.

These were not really what we were looking for, but showed that 'navigation' was a popular word.

Where Shall We Go Today?

Messages			
1-25 of 7432 matches			Page 1 of 298 Next >>
Date	Subject	Forum	Author
03/17/2000	Re: Navigation, e.g.: <--Bac	macromedia.drumbeat	James Campbell
03/17/2000	Re: Changing Page Names in N	microsoft.public.fron	Stefan B. Rusyn
03/17/2000	BMW Navigation Systems	alt.autos.bmw	Dean
03/17/2000	G4's with OS 9 and strange r	macromedia.dreamweave	David Z. Black
03/16/2000	navigation bar?	microsoft.public.publ	Raymond Giannam

All of the entries above are active links to news articles that have been posted. We clicked the subject link for article 3 and read the posting, as shown below.

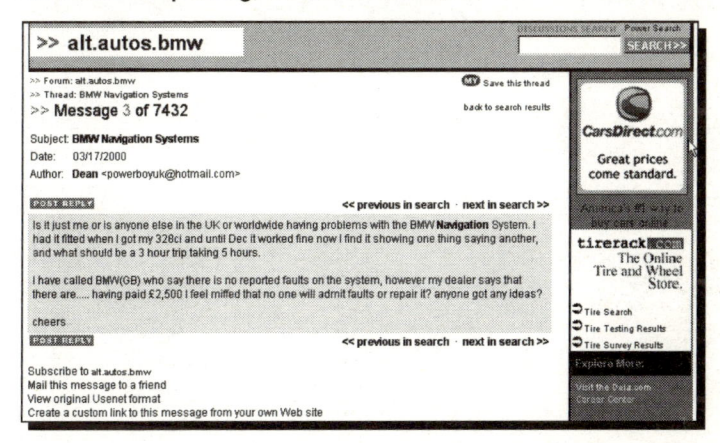

```
>> alt.autos.bmw                                      DISCUSSIONS SEARCH Power Search
                                                                        SEARCH>>
>> Forum: alt.autos.bmw
>> Thread: BMW Navigation Systems              MY  Save this thread
>> Message 3 of 7432
                                                   back to search results
Subject: BMW Navigation Systems
Date:    03/17/2000                                         CarsDirect.com
Author:  Dean <powerboyuk@hotmail.com>
                                                            Great prices
 POST REPLY          << previous in search · next in search >>   come standard.

Is it just me or is anyone else in the UK or worldwide having problems with the BMW Navigation System. I
had it fitted when I got my 328ci and until Dec it worked fine now I find it showing one thing saying another,
and what should be a 3 hour trip taking 5 hours.                                tirerack
                                                                                The Online
I have called BMW(GB) who say there is no reported faults on the system, however my dealer says that  Tire and Wheel
there are..... having paid £2,500 I feel miffed that no one will admit faults or repair it? anyone got any ideas?  Store.

cheers                                                                          Tire Search
 POST REPLY          << previous in search · next in search >>                  Tire Testing Results
                                                                                Tire Survey Results
Subscribe to alt.autos.bmw                                                      Explore More:
Mail this message to a friend
View original Usenet format                                                     Visit the Deja.com
Create a custom link to this message from your own Web site                     Career Center
```

Probably the content is not of much interest to many people in itself, but it's the principle we are trying to get over. Above and below the message are **previous** and **next** message links. You could work your way through the other messages in the retrieved listing if you wanted. **view thread** will locate any other messages in the same series, so that you can follow the whole 'conversation'.

The **post reply** option lets you actually compose and send your own message to the Usenet group, without even leaving Deja.

You can also use Deja.com to open, to read and to communicate with, your regular newsgroups. A useful facility, if you have problems with Outlook Express. In all, a very powerful facility, which is free of charge. Let's hope it stays

5 Where Shall We Go Today?

that way. Judging from the number of heavy adverts that appear on every page, we do not think that will really be too much of a problem.

We cover the newsgroups in a little more detail when covering Outlook Express in a later chapter. You may find it useful to look at the introductory text.

6

Favorites and Working Offline

Using Favorites, which are Microsoft's version of Bookmarks (their spelling, not ours!) is an easy way to access the Web pages that you need to visit on a regular basis. It is often much easier to select a page URL address from a sorted list, than to look it up and manually type it into the Address field.

Favorites

With Internet Explorer, a Favorite is simply a Windows shortcut to a Web page that the program places in the **Windows\Favorites** folder.

When you first use Internet Explorer there may already be some Favorites available for you to use. Later, as your list of regular sites grows, your Favorites menu structure will grow too. In our example here, opened by clicking the **F<u>a</u>vorites** option on the menu bar, we show how you can organise your lists of favourite bookmarks into a hierarchical list.

With Explorer 5 there are in fact two ways of accessing your list of Favorites. From the menu bar, as shown above, and by clicking the Favorites Toolbar button. The latter method opens the Favorites list into an Explorer bar on the left of the Explorer window, as shown on the next page. This bar remains open until either the Favorites Toolbar button or the X button on the top right of the Favorites bar are clicked.

69

6   Favorites and Working Offline

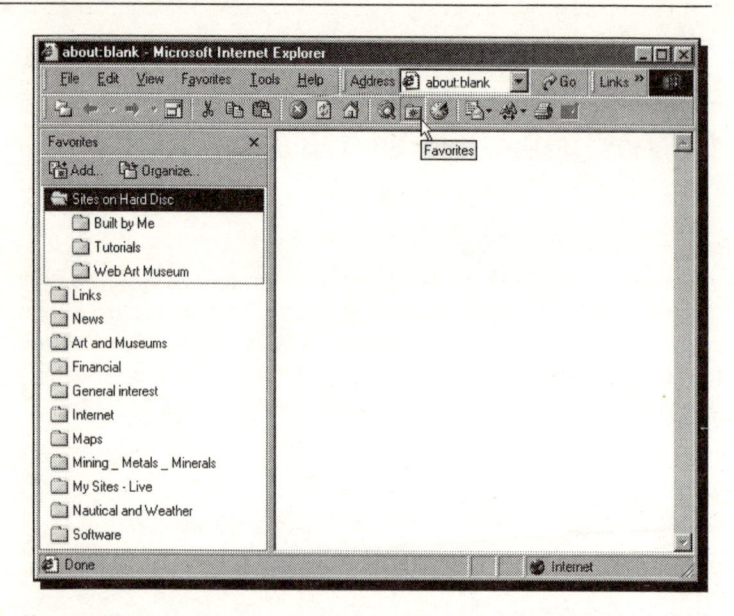

If you have a large enough monitor, or screen, you could easily work with this Favorites bar open all the time.

Adding a Favorite

There are several ways to add a Favorite to the menu. When you are viewing a Web page that you want to visit again, the easiest method is to right-click on the page and select **Add to Favorites** from the object menu, as shown here. You can also use the **Favorites**, **Add to Favorites** menu command or, if the Favorites bar is open, click its **Add** button, as shown on the facing page. All these methods start the same procedure by opening the Add Favorite dialogue box shown on the next page.

In the example we are adding a map page to our Favorite list. If your Add Favorite dialogue box does not show the list of folders, just click the **Create in** button which then

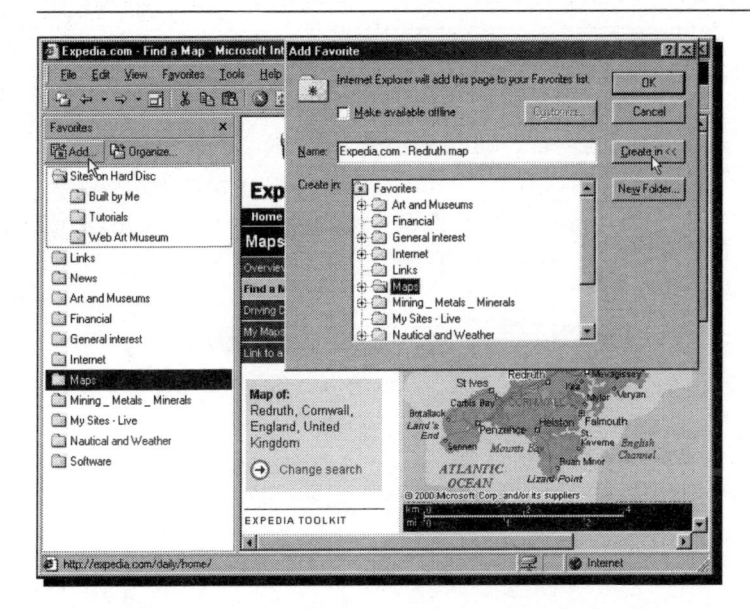

Favorites and Working Offline 6

opens the lower part of the box, for you to select a folder to receive the new Favorite. Clicking the **OK** button then completes the process.

You could also simply click the **OK** button, without selecting a folder, to add the new Favorite to the bottom of the list. It would then appear at the bottom of your **F<u>a</u>vorites** menu. The next time you open the **F<u>a</u>vorites** menu that item should be there for you to use. Each time you add a Web page like this, the page's title is offered as the name of the Favorite, but it is easy to change this in the **Name** field above, or you can rename Favorites in the Organize Favorites window as described later.

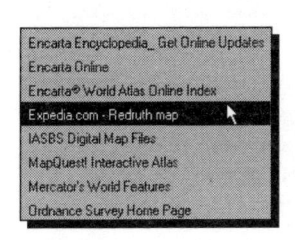

Using Favorites

To open a Web page pointed to by a Favorite, you simply open the **F<u>a</u>vorites** menu and click the item's name in the drop-down menu.

6 Favorites and Working Offline

The Organize Favorites Window

You won't have to visit many pages before your **F<u>a</u>vorites** menu will get very full and difficult to use. It is then time to tidy up a little.

You choose the **F<u>a</u>vorites**, **<u>O</u>rganize Favorites** command to open a window or dialogue box in which you can easily organise your Favorites, as shown below.

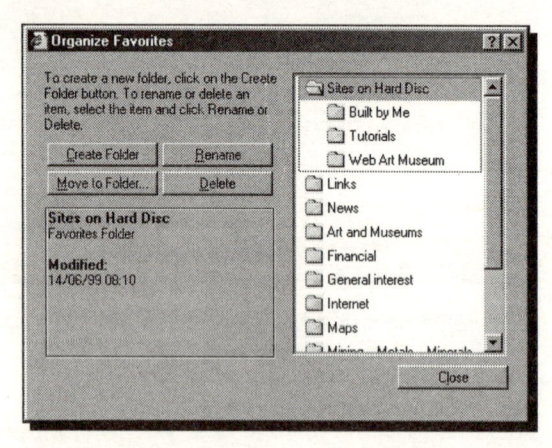

This box has changed considerably from the previous version of Internet Explorer. In Explorer 5 it is simpler, clearer and easier to use, with four buttons to **<u>R</u>ename**, **<u>D</u>elete** and **<u>M</u>ove** items or to **<u>C</u>reate** new folders, and an improved but very small navigation pane.

When you click on a folder in the list, it opens to show the sub-folders and Favorites inside it, with a 'lined box' separating the selected links from the rest of the tree (it doesn't actually take you down a level); the Info pane on the left tells you where the folder is and when you last changed it.

When you click on a Favorite, the Info pane shows you its URL, when you last visited the page and how many times you have visited it. There is also a check box for making that page available offline. All these are shown on the next page for the new map Favorite we added earlier.

Favorites and Working Offline

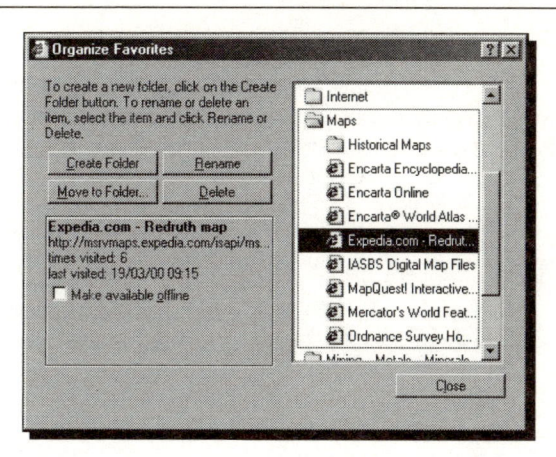

You can select any item inside the 'lined box' and carry out any of the normal Windows editing functions from a right-click menu, but remember that actions carried out on a folder also affect the contents of that folder. If you delete a folder you will lose all its contents as well! There is a fail safe though, as deleted items are actually placed in the Windows Recycle Bin, as shown below.

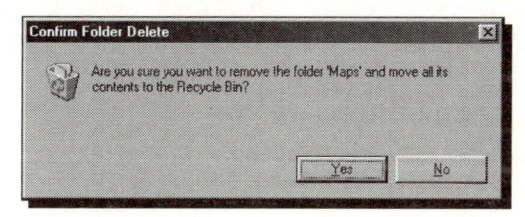

Adding a New Folder

To add a new folder simply click the **Create Folder** button which places a new folder at the end of the current 'lined box' list, type the new folder name and press the <Enter> key. You can then drag any of your existing Favorites into this folder, or nest folders by simply dragging one into another. When you drag a Favorite or folder onto a folder in the list, it opens automatically in the navigation pane, to show you any sub-folders. As you drag, an insertion bar appears between items to show you where your dragged item will be placed.

Framed Pages as Favorites

Many Web pages these days are built using a framing technique, where one page may actually contain the content of several other pages set within 'frames'. This need not worry you too much, except that older versions of browsers could not properly save a framed page as a Favorite. Instead you were always given the front page of the site, rather than the particular page on the site you wanted.

With Explorer 5 this problem has mostly been solved. When you choose a framed page to save as a Favorite, as long as you don't use the right-click menu to create the Favorite, it will be saved in the correct position in its 'frameset', and the whole framed page will open correctly when you use the Favorite. If you use the right-click menu to make your Favorite, the page address saved is for the one that was present in the frame at that time.

The page titles do not process properly though, so you will need to change the titles of the Favorites as you save them to distinguish them from any others you save on the same site, or you will have several different Favorites all with the same name!

Links Bar Favorites

You have probably seen by now, that a Links folder is automatically placed in the Favorites list. The Favorites in this folder are the ones that show on the Links bar when it is opened. You can edit its contents the same as any other folder, which lets you put an easily accessible list of special Favorites in your control area. In our example above we have put links to some of our recently produced Web sites, so that we can quickly access them to review any changes.

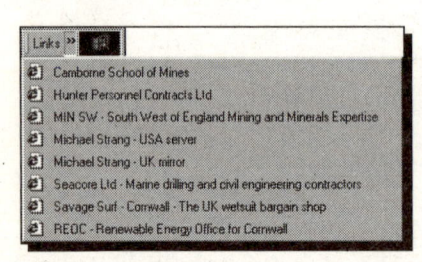

Favorites and Working Offline 6

Using Explorer Offline

Explorer 4 pioneered a way to help you keep up to date with your Web content. You could 'subscribe' to your favourite Web sites and have Explorer check them and automatically download new content to your hard disc, according to a schedule you specify. With Internet Explorer 5 this is now called working offline, as you can view these sites from your hard disc without being connected to the Internet.

With free local Internet access becoming more widely available it is theoretically possible to stay connected all the time, but the increased telephone use in the UK is rapidly slowing everything down. So for the foreseeable future working offline has some advantage.

Viewing History Pages Offline

We saw on page 51 how you could use the History bar with the **File**, **Work Offline** command and view any pages still stored in your computer's caches. If you don't want to get more formal, and are prepared to keep your History files for long periods this may be the easiest method for you to work offline. There is a better method though, using Favorites.

Offline Favorites

Setting up an offline favorite to get Explorer to make a local copy of a site or page is very easy. You just go to the page and choose **Add to Favorites** from the **Favorites** menu. Select the **Make available offline** option, as shown here. Then click the **Customize** button to open the Offline Favorite Wizard shown next.

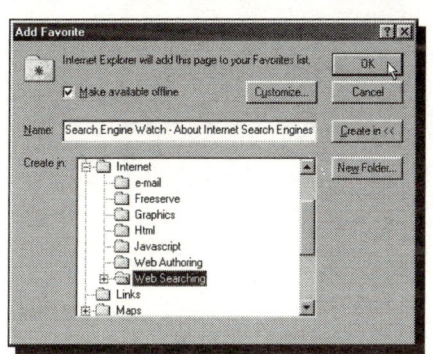

75

6 Favorites and Working Offline

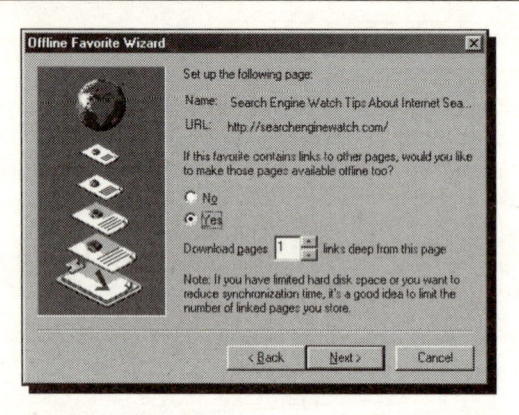

This steps you through the procedure of choosing when to update the page and how much content to download.

As you can see, this gives you the options to just download this page by selecting **No**, or to download the page and other pages linked to it. If you select **Yes** you can save whole Web sites to your hard disc. The number you select under **Download pages** controls the depth of links to download. Selecting '1' as above will download every page linked to from this Favorite. Selecting '2' will also download every page linked to from each of these pages. Be careful with this as you can easily fill your hard disc overnight!

The **Next** button opens a box in which you choose when you want to have the page 'synchronized'.

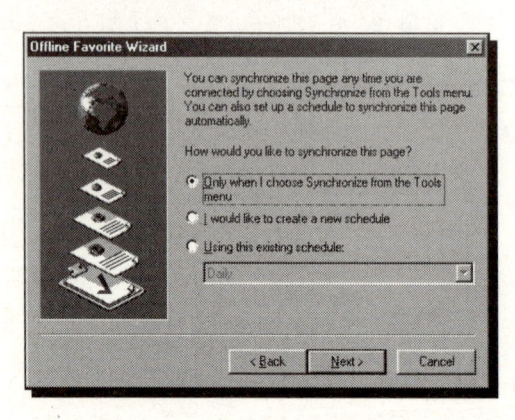

Favorites and Working Offline 6

Synchronising is simply the process of checking that your saved page content is the same as that on the Web. If not, the new Web version is downloaded for you. If you select the option **I would like to create a new schedule** and then click **Next** the box below opens.

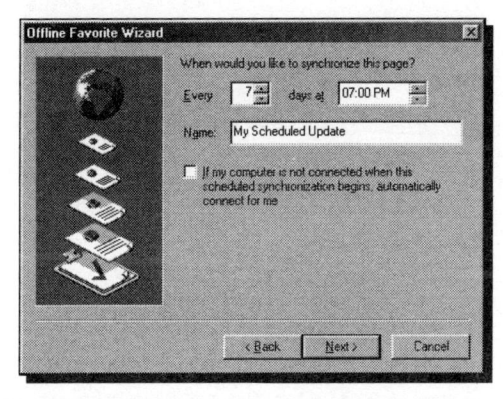

Filling this box in is self explanatory, your choices determining when Explorer will automatically synchronise the page for you.

The last box in the Wizard lets you give the password details for sites that may need them. When this is done clicking the **Finish** button will complete the wizard's operation and start the first synchronisation.

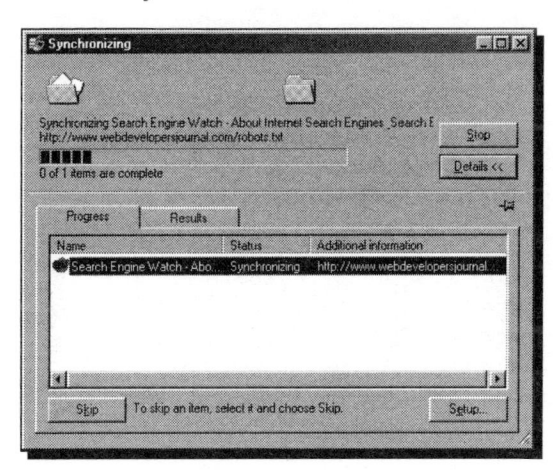

6   Favorites and Working Offline

In the future the Web page(s) on your hard disc will be updated automatically at the frequency you set, as long as your computer is actually switched on and connected at the time. If you use a modem connection, you may want to carry out this operation yourself with the **Tools**, **Synchronize** menu command, as shown below. The choice is yours.

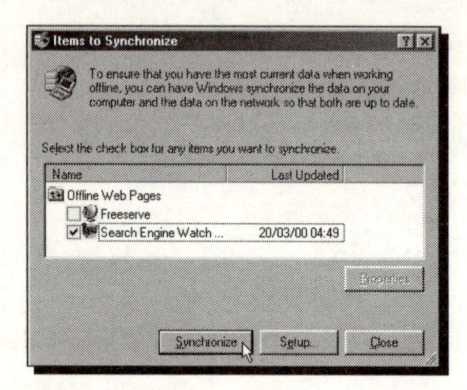

Working Offline

In the future, to view the saved pages without being connected to the Internet, use the **File**, **Work Offline** menu command, click the Favorites Toolbar button to open the Favorites bar and find the shortcut link in the list, as below.

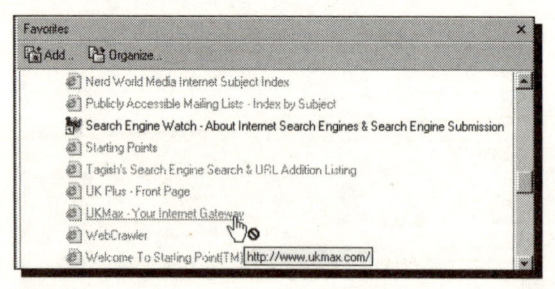

In this list the newly saved Favorite shows in bold, whereas all the other links are 'greyed out' as they are not available for offline viewing. Clicking the 'Search Engine Watch' link will open that page immediately. To open any of the other Favorites in the list you will have to connect to the Internet.

Favorite Properties

Every Favorite has a set of properties which you can edit quite easily from its Properties box, which is best opened for the first time from the Organize Favorites box.

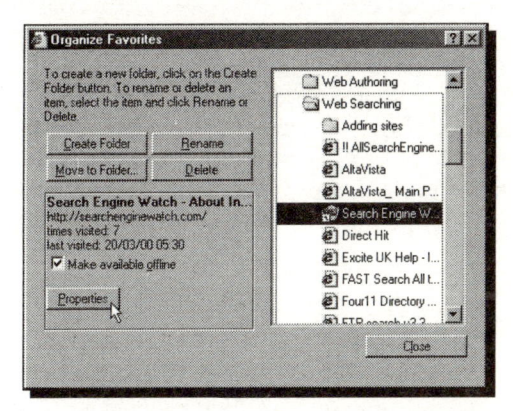

To do this, ensure the **Make available o̲ffline** option is selected, as shown above, and click the **P̲roperties** button.

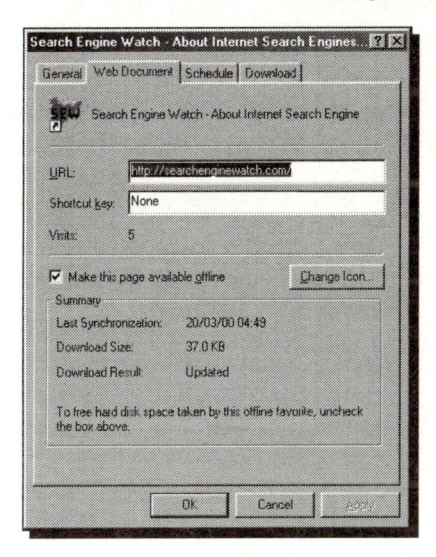

6 Favorites and Working Offline

As shown, this set of Properties sheets gives you complete control of the Favorite and, as long as it has been selected for offline viewing, of its synchronisation schedule.

From the Schedule tabbed sheet you can choose for either manual or scheduled updates. From the Download tabbed sheet you can choose the update time and interval (1 to 99 days) and tell Explorer whether to dial up if you're not already connected to the Internet. Don't forget that your PC will still need to be switched on! You can also choose how many levels of links to follow on the page, and whether to limit this to the same Web server or to set a size limit on the download.

The Advanced button lets you select any page elements you don't want to download, such as images, sound, video, ActiveX or Java components.

We will leave it to you to explore the further possibilities here. The big advantage of working offline is that once a page, or pages, have been downloaded and saved on your computer, you can view them all without even being connected to the Internet, by using the **File**, **Work Offline** command. This not only saves your phone bill if you use a modem, but also means the pages load up almost instantly.

Once a Favorite has been set up, the easiest way to control it is to right-click on it in the Favorite list, select **Properties** from the menu that is opened and make any changes you want in the Properties box that is opened.

7

E-mail with Outlook Express 5

Internet Explorer 5 comes with the very powerful mail and news facility, Outlook Express 5, built into it, which makes it very easy for you to send and receive e-mail messages. We are impressed with Outlook Express and use it for our e-mail correspondence.

What is E-mail

E-mail, or electronic mail, is cheaper, quicker, and usually much easier to prepare and send than Post Office mail. So what is an e-mail? It's simply an electronic message sent between computers which can include attachments like pictures, document files or Web pages. The message is passed from one computer to another as it travels through the Internet, with each computer reading its e-mail address and routing it further until it reaches its destination, where it is stored in a 'mailbox'. This usually only takes a few minutes, and sometimes only seconds.

You can use e-mail for keeping in touch with friends and family and for professional reasons. You can send e-mail to most people, anywhere in the world, as long as they have their own e-mail address. These days all Internet service providers offer an e-mail address and mailbox facility to all their customers.

To retrieve your e-mail messages you have to contact your mailbox, download them to your PC, and then read and process them (just like any other mail). As we shall see, Outlook Express makes this whole procedure very easy and takes most of the mystery out of the whole e-mail process.

E-mail Addresses

An e-mail address usually has two main parts, which are separated with the '@' character, and usually contain at least one dot (the '.' character). The following is a typical, if short, example.

aperson@organisation.co.uk

The part before the @ is the user name which identifies him, or her, at the mailbox. This user name is usually made up from the name and initials of the user.

After the @ comes the domain name, which identifies the computer where the person has a mailbox and is usually the name of a company, a university, or other organisation. There is a central register of these domain names, as each must be unique. When you set up your account, you can sometimes get your service provider to customise a domain name for you, at a price, of course. Otherwise you will probably use the domain name of the service provider itself.

Next, there's a '.' or dot, followed by two, or three, letters that indicate the type of domain it is. In our example above this is **.co** which means the host is a business or commercial enterprise, located in the United Kingdom (**.uk**). In the USA, or anywhere else for that matter, this would be **.com** instead, but not followed by a country identifier.

A host name ending with **.edu** means the host is a US university or educational facility. A UK university would be **.ac.uk**. A **.org** indicates the host is a US non-commercial organisation.

Some of the more common extensions you might encounter are:

edu	Educational sites in the US
com	Commercial sites worldwide
gov	Government sites in the US
net	Network administrative organisations
mil	Military sites in the US

org	Organisations in the US that don't fit into other categories
fr	France
ca	Canada
uk	United Kingdom
**	Other county codes

Once you get used to these address parts, they begin to make more sense. For example, the writer's e-mail address is

prmolive@csm.ex.ac.uk

This reads quite easily as:

PRM Oliver located at Camborne School of Mines, part of the University of Exeter, which is an academic institution in the UK.

So if you know where somebody works you can even make an attempt to guess his, or her, e-mail address. A home address obtained through a commercial Internet provider would not be very easy though.

7 E-mail with Outlook Express 5

Outlook Express

There are several ways to start the Outlook Express program, you can click the Desktop icon shown here, or the small icon on the left of the Windows Taskbar. Also like the other Works 2000 applications you can use the Task Launcher, by selecting **Outlook Express** in the **Programs** window list and then clicking the **Start Outlook Express** link. In all these cases a window something like ours below should be opened.

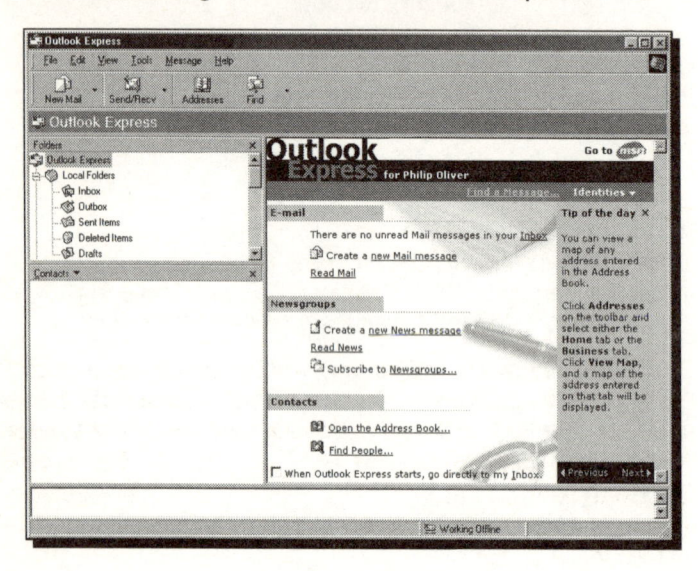

Connecting to your Server

Before you can use Outlook Express to send, or receive, mail you have to tell the program how to connect to your server's facilities. You do this by completing your personal e-mail connection details in the Internet Connection Wizard shown here, which opens when you first attempt to use the Read Mail facility.

E-mail with Outlook Express 5

The other way to enter this Wizard, if it does not open, or if you want to change your connection details, is to use the **Tools**, **Accounts** menu command, select the mail tab and click **Add**, followed by **Mail**.

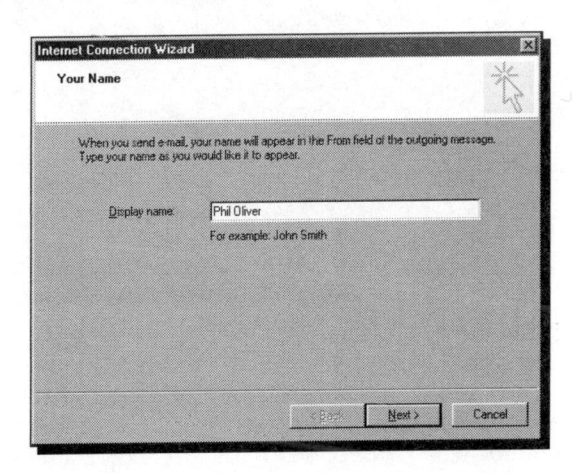

Type your name in the first box, as shown above, and click the **Next** button to open the second box. Enter your e-mail address in this box, if you have not organised one yet you could always check the **I'd like to sign up for a new account from Hotmail** option. Hotmail is a free browser-based e-mail service now owned by Microsoft. Hence its inclusion!

In the third dialogue box enter your e-mail server details, as shown for us, on the next page. To complete some of the details here you may need to ask your Internet service provider, or system administrator, for help.

7 E-mail with Outlook Express 5

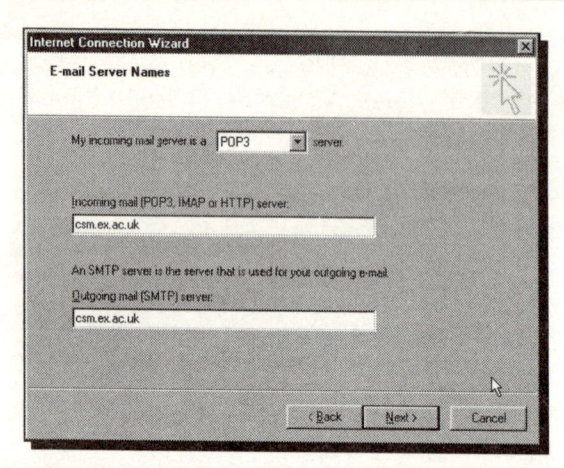

The details shown above will obviously only work for the writer, so please don't try them! In the next box enter your log-in name and password. Details of these should have been given to you by your Internet service provider or system administrator when you opened your 'service account'. You have now completed the Wizard so press **Finish** to return you to the Internet Accounts box, with your new account set up as shown below for us.

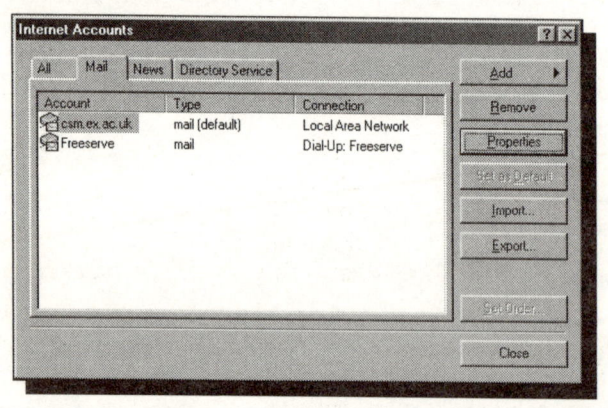

In the future, selecting the account in this box and clicking the **Properties** button will give you access to the settings sheets to check, or change, your details. We changed the Connection settings here to LAN (local area network).

E-mail with Outlook Express 5

Once your connection is established, you can click the Read Mail coloured link, or the **Inbox** entry in the Folder List on the left side of the Outlook Express 5 opening window. Both of these actions open the Inbox, which when opened for the first time, will probably contain a message from Microsoft, like that shown below.

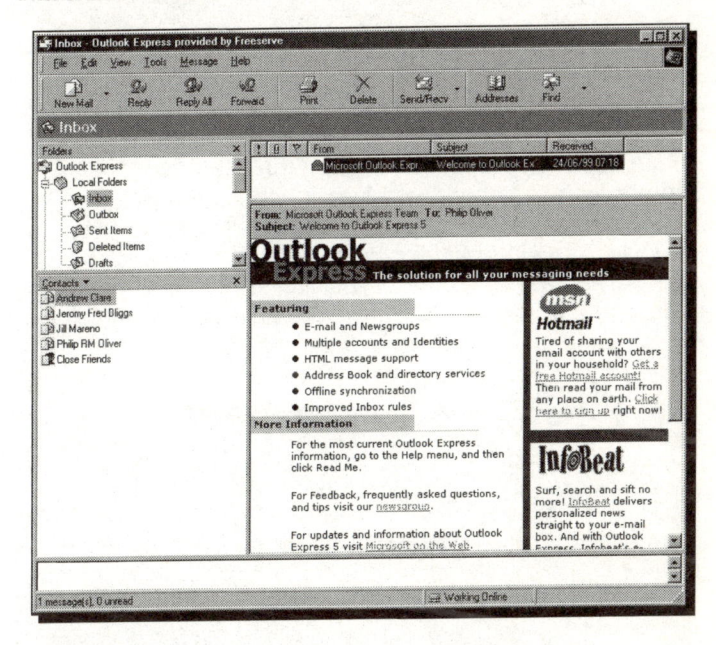

This shows the default Outlook Express Main window layout, which consists of a Folder List to the left with a Contacts list from the Address Book below it, a Message List to the right and a Preview Pane below that. The Folder List contains all the active mail folders, news servers and newsgroups.

Clicking on one of these places its contents in the Message List, and clicking on a message opens a Preview of it below for you to see. Double-clicking on a message opens the message in its own window.

7 E-mail with Outlook Express 5

To check your mail, click the Send/Recv Toolbar icon which will download any new messages from your mailbox to your hard disc. You can then read and process your mail at your leisure without necessarily being still connected to the Internet.

A Trial Run

Before explaining in more detail the main features of Outlook Express we will step through the procedure of sending a very simple e-mail message. The best way to test out any unfamiliar e-mail features is to send a test message to your own e-mail address. This saves wasting somebody else's time, and the message can be very quickly checked to see the results.

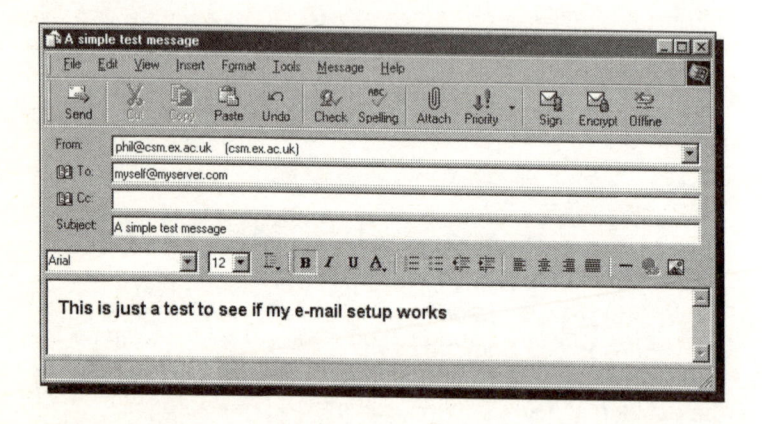

Click the New Mail icon and select **No Stationery** to open the New Message window, shown above.

Type your own e-mail address in the **To:** field, and a title for the message in the **Subject:** field. The text in this subject field will form a header for the message when it is received, so it helps to show in a few words what the message is about. Type your message and when you are happy with it, click the Send toolbar icon.

By default, your mesage is stored in an Outbox folder, and pressing the Send/Recv Toolbar icon will send it, hopefully straight into your mailbox. When Outlook Express next checks for mail, it will find the message and download it into the Inbox folder, for you to read and enjoy!

The Main Window

After the initial opening window, Outlook Express uses three other main windows, which we will refer to as; the Main window which opens next; the Read Message window for reading your mail; and the New Message window, to compose your outgoing mail messages.

The Main window consists of a Toolbar, a menu, and five panes with the default display shown in our example on page 18. You can choose different pane layouts, and customise the Toolbar, with the **View**, **Layout** menu command, but we will let you try these for yourself.

The Folders List

The folders pane contains a list of your mail folders, your news servers and any newsgroups you have subscribed to. There are always at least five mail folders, as shown in our example on the next page. You can add your own with the **File**, **Folder**, **New** menu command from the Main window. We added 'My new folder' like this. You can delete them again with the **File**, **Folder**, **Delete** command. These operations can also be carried out after right-clicking a folder in the list. You can drag messages from the Message List and drop them into any of the folders, to 'store' them there.

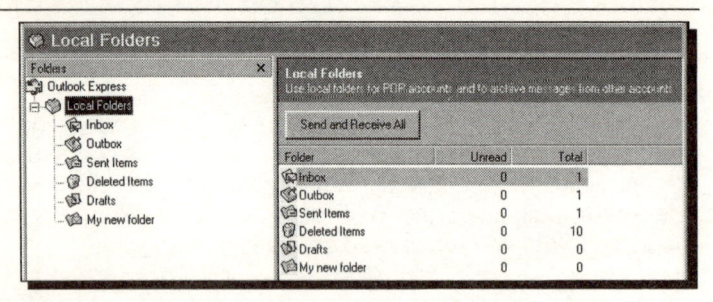

7   E-mail with Outlook Express 5

Note the icons shown above, any new folders you add will have the same icon as that of our added one above.

The Contacts Pane

This pane simply lists the contacts held in your Address Book. Double-clicking on an entry in this list opens a New Message window with the message already addressed to that person.

The Message List

When you select a folder, by clicking it in the Folders list, the Message list shows the contents of that folder. Brief details of each message are displayed on one line.

The first column shows the message priority, if any, the second shows whether the message has an attachment, and the third shows whether the message has been 'flagged'. All of these are indicated by icons on the message line, like our example to the left. The 'From' column shows the message status icon (listed on the next page) and the name of the sender, 'Subject' shows the title of each mail message, and 'Received' shows the date it reached you. You can control what columns display in this pane with the **View**, **Columns** menu command.

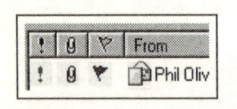

To sort a list of messages, you can click the mouse pointer in the title of the column you want the list sorted on, clicking it again will sort it in reverse order. The sorted column is shown with a triangle mark.

Message Status Icons

This icon	Indicates this
0	The message has one or more files attached.
!	The message has been marked high priority by the sender.
↓	The message has been marked low priority by the sender.
◿	The message has been read. The message heading appears in light type.
✉	The message has not been read. The message heading appears in bold type.
◿	The message has been replied to.
◿	The message has been forwarded.
◿	The message is in progress in the Drafts folder.
◿	The message is digitally signed and unopened.
◿	The message is encrypted and unopened.
◿	The message is digitally signed, encrypted and unopened.
◿	The message is digitally signed and has been opened.
◿	The message is encrypted and has been opened.
◿	The message is digitally signed and encrypted, and has been opened.
⊞	The message has responses that are collapsed. Click the icon to show all the responses (expand the conversation).
⊟	The message and all of its responses are expanded. Click the icon to hide all the responses (collapse the conversation).
▽	The unread message header is on an IMAP server.
✗	The opened message is marked for deletion on an IMAP server.
⚑	The message is flagged.
↓	The IMAP message is marked to be downloaded.
⊞↓	The IMAP message and all conversations are marked to be downloaded.
⊟↓	The individual IMAP message (without conversations) is marked to be downloaded.

The Preview Pane

When you select a message in the Message list, by clicking it once, it is displayed in the Preview pane, which takes up the rest of the window. This lets you read the first few lines to see if the message is worth bothering with. If so, double clicking the header, in the Message list, will open the message in the Read Message window, as shown later in the chapter.

You could use the Preview pane to read all your mail, especially if your messages are all on the short side, but it is easier to process them from the Read Message window.

7   E-mail with Outlook Express 5

The Main Window Toolbar

New Mail — Opens the New Message window for creating a new mail message, with the To: field blank.

Reply — Opens the New Message window for replying to the current mail message, with the To: field pre-addressed to the original sender. The original Subject field is prefixed with Re:.

Reply All — Opens the New Message window for replying to the current mail message, with the To: field pre-addressed to all that received copies of the original message. The original Subject field is prefixed with Re:.

Forward — Opens the New Message window for forwarding the current mail message. The To: field is blank. The original Subject field is prefixed with Fw:.

Print — Prints the selected message.

Delete — Deletes the currently selected message and places it in the Deleted Items folder.

Send/Recv — Connects to the mailbox server and downloads waiting messages, which it places in the Inbox folder. Sends any messages waiting in the Outbox folder.

Addresses — Opens the Address Book.

Find — Finds a message or an e-mail address using Find People facilities of the Address Book.

The Read Message Window

If you double-click a message in the Message list of the Main window the Read Message window is opened, as shown below.

This is the best window to read your mail in. It has its own menu system and Toolbar, which lets you rapidly process and move between the messages in a folder.

The Read Message Toolbar

This window has its own Toolbar, but only two icons are different from those in the Main window.

Previous - Displays the previous mail message in the Read Message window. The button appears depressed if there are no previous messages.

Next - Displays the next mail message in the Read Message window. The button appears depressed if there are no more messages.

Viewing File Attachments

Until fairly recently, e-mail on the Internet was good only for short text notes. You couldn't send attachments like formatted document or graphic files with your messages. That changed with the advent of MIME, which stands for Multipurpose Internet Mail Extension. With Outlook Express you can send Web pages, other formatted documents, photos, sound and video files as attachments to your main e-mail message, and some of them as part of the actual message itself.

One thing to be careful of though, is to make sure that the person you are sending your message to has e-mail software capable of decoding them. In our experience many people seem to stick to their tried and trusted 'old' e-mail software that does not.

A file attachment appears at the bottom of the message in the Read Message window. To save the attachment, use the **File**, **Save Attac**h**ments** menu command, or right-click the attachment and select the **Save As** option.

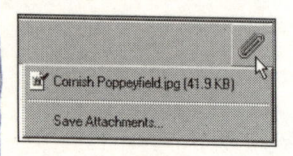

To display, or run, an attachment from the preview pane, click the paper-clip file attachment icon in the preview pane header, and then click the file name. You may get a virus warning here, but if you are happy about the document source just carry on. To save the attachment click the **Save Attachments** button that is opened, as shown above.

The New Message Window

We briefly looked into the New Message window earlier in the chapter. This is the window, shown next, that you will use to create any messages you want to send electronically from Outlook Express. It is important to understand its features, so that you can get the most out of it.

E-mail with Outlook Express 5

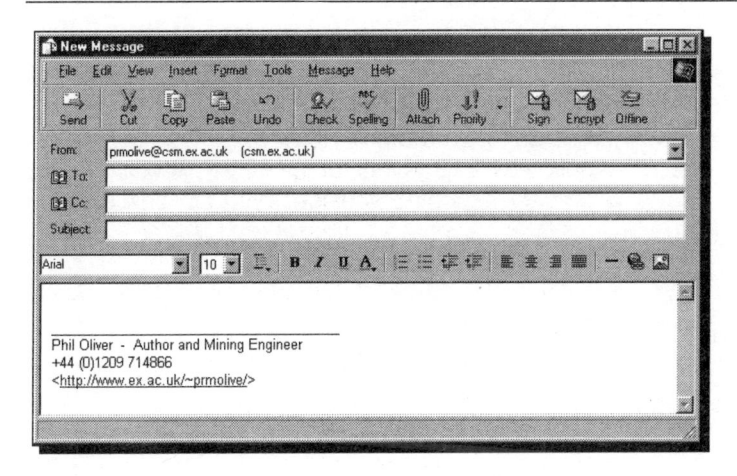

As we saw, this window can be opened by using the New Mail Toolbar icon from the Main window, as well as the **Message**, **New Message** menu command. From other windows you can also use the **Message**, **New** command, or the <Ctrl+N> keyboard shortcut. The newly opened window has its own menu system and Toolbar, which let you rapidly prepare and send your new e-mail messages.

Message Stationery

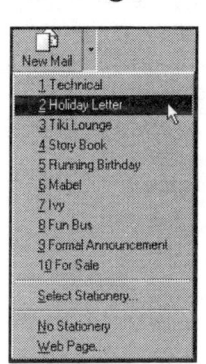

Another Outlook Express feature is that it lets you send your messages on pre-formatted stationery for added effect, as in our example on the next page.

To access these, click the down arrow next to the New Mail button in the Main window and either select from the **1** to **10** list, as shown here, or use the **Select Stationery** command to open a box with many more stationery types on offer.

To send a plain message, with no 'fancy' effects, use the **No Stationery** option.

95

7 E-mail with Outlook Express 5

> Dear friends,
>
> Happy Christmas from all in Cornwall
>
> Phil Oliver - Author and Mining Engineer
> +44 (0)1209 714866
> < http://www.ex.ac.uk/~prmolive/ >

The New Message Toolbar

Send Message - Sends message, either to the recipient, or to the Outbox folder.

Cut - Cuts selected text to the Windows clipboard.

Copy - Copies selected text to the Windows clipboard.

Paste - Pastes the contents of the Windows clipboard into the current message.

Undo - Undoes the last editing action.

Check Names - Checks that names match your entries in the address book, or are in correct e-mail address format.

E-mail with Outlook Express 5

Spelling - Checks the spelling of the current message before it is sent.

Attach File - Opens the Insert Attachment window for you to select a file to be attached to the current message.

Set Priority - Sets the message priority as high or low, to indicate its importance to the recipient.

Digitally sign message - Adds a digital signature to the message to confirm to the recipient that it is from you.

Encrypt message - Encodes the message so that only the recipient can read it.

Work Offline - Closes connection to the Internet so that you can process your mail offline. The button then changes to **Work Online**.

Your Own Signature

If you have created a signature from the Main window in the **Tools**, **Options**, **Signature** tabbed box, as shown at the top of the next page, its text is automatically placed for you at the end of the message creation area.

You could also create a more fancy signature file in a text editor like Notepad, or WordPad, including the text and characters you want added to all your messages, and point to it in the **File** section of this box. We have chosen to **Add signatures to all outgoing messages**, but you could leave this option blank and use the **Insert**, **Signature** command from the New Message window menu system if you prefer.

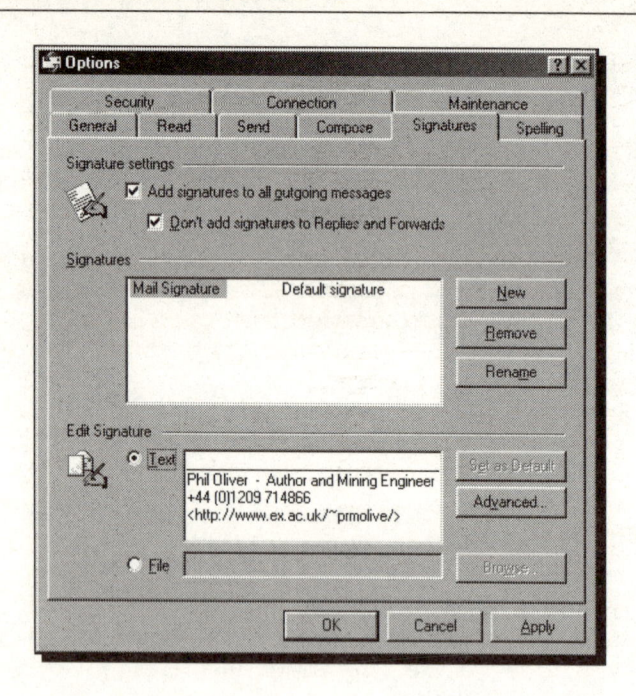

Message Formatting

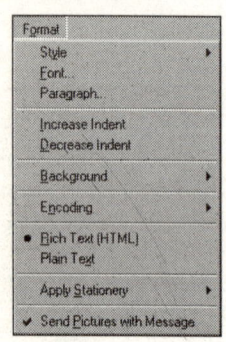

Outlook Express provides quite sophisticated formatting options for an e-mail editor from both the **Format** menu and Toolbar. These only work if you prepare the message in HTML format, as used in Web documents. In the **Tools**, **Options**, **Send** box you can set this to be your default mail sending format.

To use the format for the current message only, select **Rich Text (HTML)** from the **Format** menu, as we have done here. If **Plain Text** is selected, the black dot will be placed against this option on the menu, and the formatting features will not then be available.

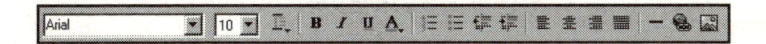

The above Format Toolbar is added to the New Message window when you are in HTML mode and all the **Format** menu options are then made active.

All of the formatting features are well covered elsewhere in the book so we will not repeat them now. Most of them are quite well demonstrated in Microsoft's opening message to you. You should be able to prepare some very easily readable e-mail messages with these features, but remember that not everyone will be able to read the work in the way that you spent hours creating. Only e-mail programs that support MIME (Multipurpose Internet Mail Extensions) can read HTML formatting. When your recipient's e-mail program does not read HTML, the message appears as plain text with an HTML file attached.

At the risk of being called boring we think it is usually better to stick to plain text, not only can everyone read it, but it is much quicker to transmit and use.

Adding Attachments

If you want to send a Web page, or other type of file as an attachment to your main e-mail message you simply click the Insert File Toolbar button and select the file to attach. This opens the Insert Attachment dialogue box, for you to select the file, or files, you want to go with your message.

The attached files are shown in a special 'Attach:' section in the message header, as shown below.

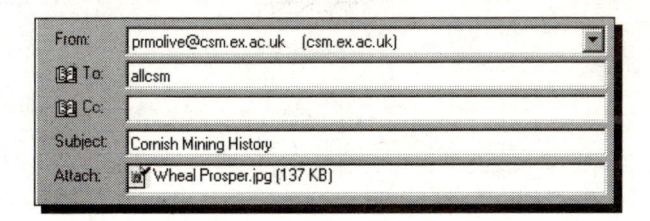

Sending E-mail Messages

When you have filled in the address fields, typed and formatted the body of your message, added any attachments, and maybe placed a signature, you simply click the Send Toolbar icon, shown here, to start the transmission process. What happens to the message next depends on your settings.

If you have a dial-up connection (using a modem) you may want to keep the message and transmit it later, maybe with several others to save on your telephone bill. In that case, make sure the **Send messages immediately** option is not selected in the **Tools**, **Options**, **Send** settings box. Clicking the above Send Toolbar icon will then place the message in the Outbox folder.

When you are ready to send your held messages you click the Send/Recv Toolbar icon on the Main window. If you forget to do this, Outlook Express will prompt you with a message box when you attempt to exit the program.

When the **Send messages immediately** option is selected, your messages will be sent on their way as soon as you click the Send Toolbar button. This option is best used if you have a permanent connection to the Internet, or your e-mail is being sent over an internal network, or Intranet.

Replying to a Message

When you receive an e-mail message that you want to reply to, Outlook Express makes it very easy to do. The reply address and the new message subject fields are both added automatically for you. Also, by default, the original message is quoted in the reply window for you to edit as required.

With the message you want to reply to still open, either click the Reply to Sender Toolbar icon, use the **Message**, **Reply to Sender** menu command, or use the <Ctrl+R> keyboard shortcut. All these actions open the New Message window and the message you are replying to will, by default, be placed under the insertion point.

With long messages, you should not leave all of the original text in your reply. This can be bad practice, which rapidly makes new messages very large and time consuming to download. You should usually edit the quoted text, so that it is obvious what you are referring to. One or two lines may even be enough.

Removing Deleted Messages

Whenever you delete a message it is actually moved to the Deleted Items folder. If ignored, this folder gets bigger and bigger over time, so you need to check it every few days and manually re-delete messages you are sure you will not need again, in which case you are given a last warning message.

If you are confident that you will not need this safety net, you can opt to **Empty messages from the 'Deleted Items' folder on exit** in the **Tools**, **Options**, **Maintenance** settings box, opened from the Main window. You will then have a short time to change your mind before they are finally deleted.

Organising your Messages

Perhaps most of the e-mail messages you get will have no 'long term' value and will be simply deleted once you have dealt with them. Some however you may well need to keep for future reference. After a few weeks it can be surprising how many of these messages can accumulate. If you don't do something with them they seem to take over and slow the whole process down. That is the reason for the Folders List.

7 E-mail with Outlook Express 5

As we saw earlier you can open and close new folders in this area, and can move and copy messages from one folder into another.

To move a message, you just select its header line in the Message List and with the left mouse button depressed 'drag' it to the folder in the Folders List, as shown to the left. When you release the mouse button, the message will be moved to that folder.

The copy procedure is very much the same, except you must also have the <Ctrl> key depressed when you release the mouse button. You can tell which operation is taking place by looking at the mouse pointer. It will show a '+' when copying, as on the right.

The System Folders

Outlook Express has five folders which it always keeps intact and will not let you delete. Some of these we have met already.

The *Inbox* holds all incoming messages. You should delete or move messages from this folder as soon as you have read them.

The *Outbox* holds messages that have been prepared but not yet transmitted. As soon as the messages are sent they are automatically removed to the *Sent Items* folder. You can then decide whether to 'file' your copies of these messages, or whether to delete them. As we saw on the last page, any messages you do delete are placed in the *Deleted Items* folder as a safety feature.

The last system folder is the *Drafts* folder, which does not seem to be mentioned at all in Microsoft's program information. If you close a message without sending it, Outlook Express will ask you to save it in this folder. We also use the Drafts folder to store our message pro-formas and unfinished messages that will need more work before they can be sent.

8

Some Other E-mail Features

Outlook Express Help

Outlook Express has a built-in Help system, which is accessed with the **Help**, **Contents and Index** menu command, or the **F1** function key. These open a Windows 98 type Help window, as shown below.

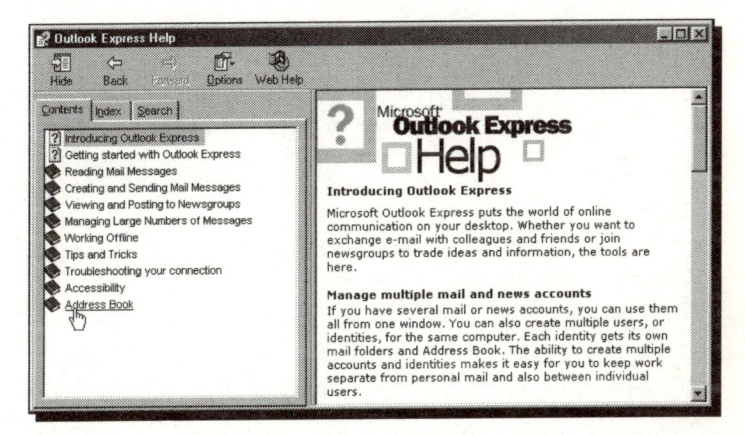

We strongly recommend that you work your way through all the items listed in the **Contents** tabbed section. Clicking on a closed book icon will open it and display a listing of its contents. Double-clicking on a list item will then open a window with a few lines of Help information.

Another way of browsing the Help system is to click the **Index** tab and work your way through the alphabetic listing. The **Search** tab opens a search facility you can use, as shown next. In this example we typed 'check spelling' in the **Type in the keyword to find** text field and clicked the **List**

8   Some Other E-mail Features

Topics button. Then, selecting one of the **Topic**s found and clicking **Display**, opened Help information on it, with the words searched-for highlighted, as shown below.

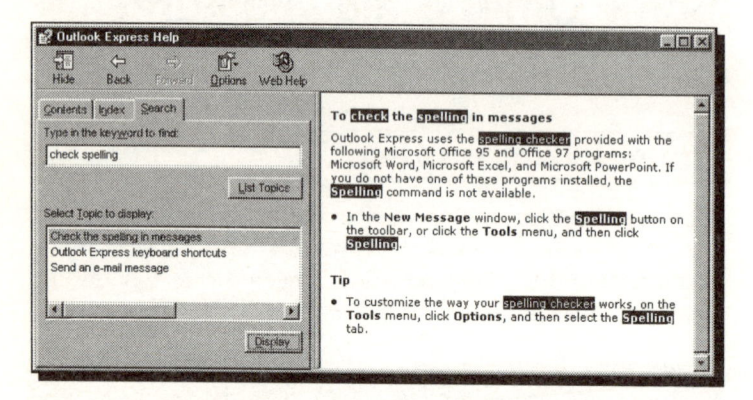

If you want to copy any of the text displayed, you will first have to use the **Options**, **Search Highlight Off** command, then select the text you want, right-click it, and select **Copy** from the opened menu. If you are connected, the Web Help icon accesses the Support Online from Microsoft Technical Support which can give more specific help with the program, though we have not tried it.

The Help provided by Microsoft with Outlook Express 5, is a big improvement over some earlier versions, and it is well worth spending an hour or two getting to grips with it. There still seem to be some glaring omissions though!

Spell Checking

Many of the e-mail messages we receive seem to be full of errors and spelling mistakes. Some people do not seem to read their work before clicking the 'Send' button. With Outlook Express this should be a thing of the past, as the program is linked to the spell checker that comes with other Microsoft programs. If you do not have any of these, the option will not be available to you, though.

Some Other E-mail Features 8

To try it out, prepare a message in the New Message window, but make an obvious spelling mistake, maybe like ours below. Pressing the Spelling Toolbar button, the **F7** function key, or using the **Tools**, **Spelling** command, will start the process.

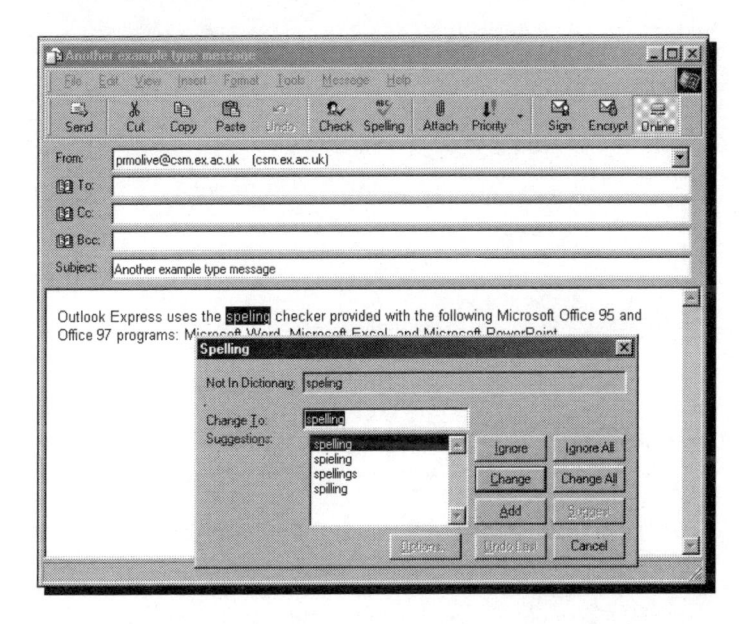

Any words not recognised by the checker will be flagged up as above. If you are happy with the word just click one of the **Ignore** buttons, if not, you can type a correction in the **Change To** field, or accept one of the **Suggestions**, and then click the **Change** button. With us the **Options** button always seemed 'greyed out', but you can get some control over the spell checker on the settings sheet opened from the main Outlook Express menu with the **Tools**, **Options** command, and then clicking the **Spelling** tab.

The available options, as shown on the next page, are self explanatory so we will not dwell on them. If you want every message to be checked before it is sent, make sure you select the **Always check spelling before sending** option.

8 Some Other E-mail Features

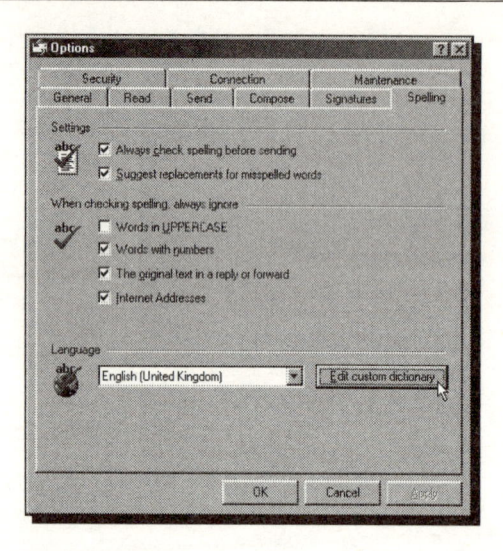

Connection at Start-Up

While you are looking at the program settings, open the **Tools**, **Options**, **Connection** tabbed sheet, shown below. This gives you some control of what happens when you open Outlook Express, depending on your connection settings for Internet Explorer. If you have a modem connection to the Internet, it can be annoying when a program goes into dial-up mode unexpectedly.

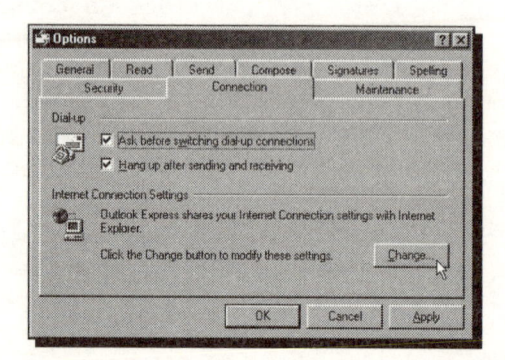

Some Other E-mail Features   8

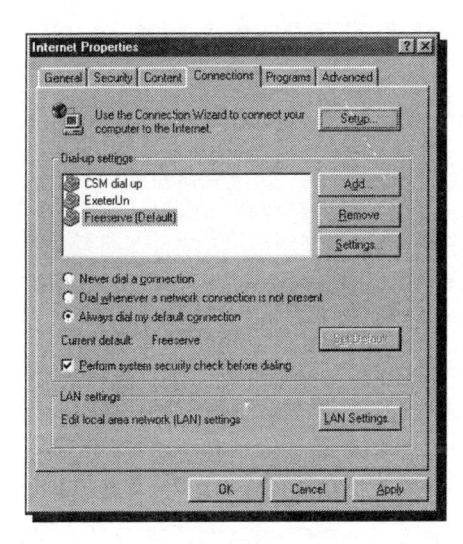

As it stands above, we would be connected to our 'Freeserve' mailbox whenever we started Outlook Express. With a permanent Internet connection this would be fine, but with a modem connection, we prefer to have the above **Never dial a connection** option selected. Then when we are ready to 'go on line', as long as we have not selected **Work Offline** as a **File** menu option, we simply click the Send/Recv toolbar icon shown here. If you have more than one Internet connection, the down arrow to the right of the icon lets you select which one to use.

Printing your Messages

It was originally thought by some, that computers would lead to the paperless office. That has certainly not proved to be correct. It seems that however good our electronic communication media becomes most people want to see the results printed on paper. As far as books are concerned, long may that last!

8 Some Other E-mail Features

Outlook Express 5 lets you print e-mail messages to paper, but it does not give you any control over the page settings it uses. You can, however, alter the font size of your printed output as it depends on the font size you set for viewing your messages. As shown here, you have five 'relative' size options available from the **View**, **T**e**xt Size** menu command.

When you are ready to print a message in the Read Message window, use the <Ctrl+P> key combination, or the **File**, **Print** menu command, to open the Print dialogue box shown below.

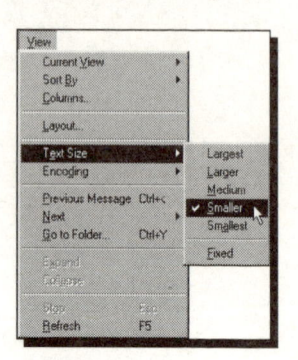

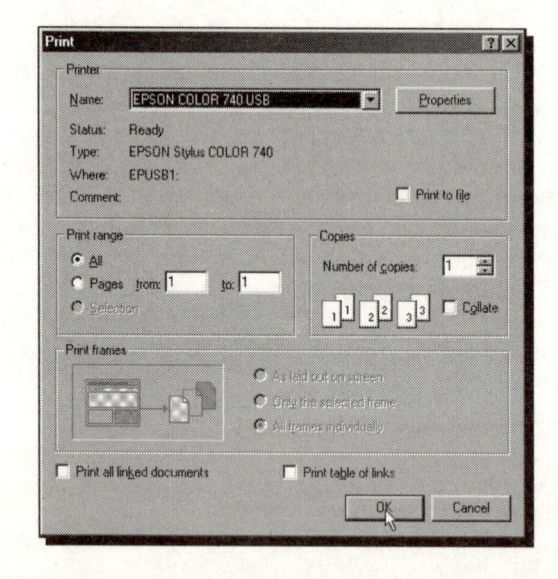

Make sure the correct printer **Name** and **Properties** are selected, choose the pages to be printed, how many copies you want, and finally click **OK** to start the printing process. You can also click the Print toolbar icon shown here to start the printing procedure.

If the message has Web page links on it, there are two features in the above dialogue box, as when printing from the Internet Explorer browser:

- The **Print ta<u>b</u>le of links** option, which when checked, gives a hard copy listing of the URL addresses of all the links present in the page.

- The **Print all lin<u>k</u>ed documents** option, which not only prints the message, but all the Web pages linked to it.

The Address Book

E-mail addresses are often quite complicated and not at all easy to remember. With Outlook Express there is a very useful Address Book built in and an almost empty example of one is shown here.

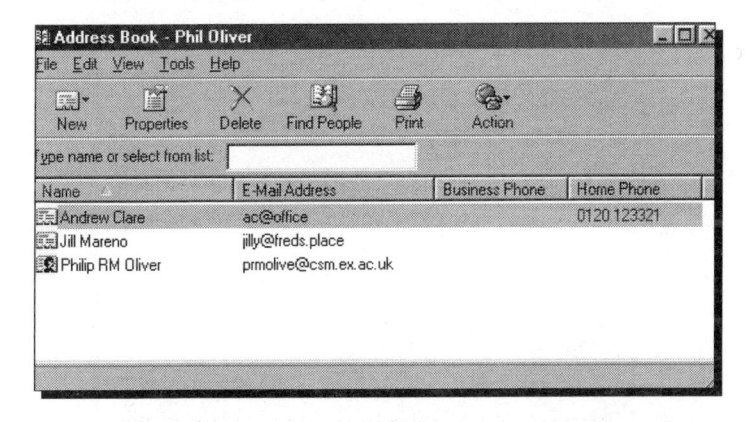

It can be opened from the Main window by clicking the Address Book Toolbar icon, or using the **<u>T</u>ools**, **Address <u>B</u>ook** menu command.

Once in the Address Book, you can manually add a person's full details and e-mail address, in the Properties box

8 Some Other E-mail Features

that opens when you click the New Toolbar icon and select **New Contact**, as shown here. Selecting **New Group** from this drop-down menu lets you create a grouping of e-mail addresses, you can then send mail to everyone in the group with one operation.

To send a new message to anyone listed in your Address Book, open a New Message window and use the **Tools**, **Select Recipients** command, or click on any of the To, Cc, or Bcc icons shown here on the right.

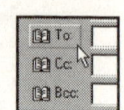

In the Select Recipients box which is opened, you can select a person's name and click either the **To:->** button to place it in the **To:** field of your message, the **Cc->** button to place it in the **Cc:** field, or the **Bcc->** button to place it in the **Bcc:** field.

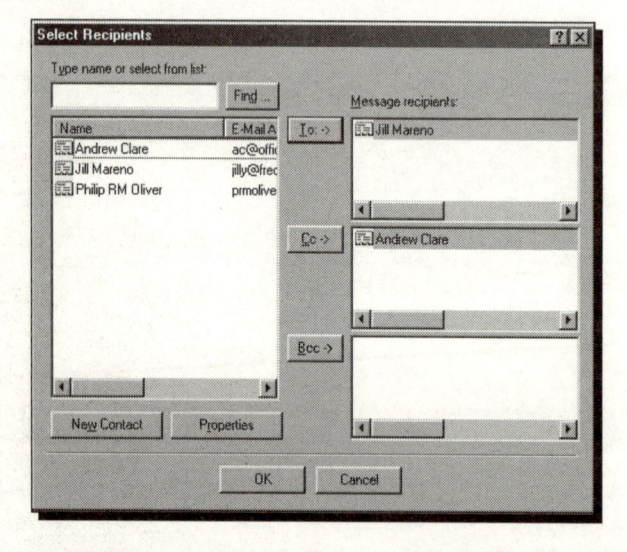

The **New Contact** button lets you add details for a new person to the Address Book, and the **Properties** button lets you edit an existing entry, as shown on the facing page.

Some Other E-mail Features 8

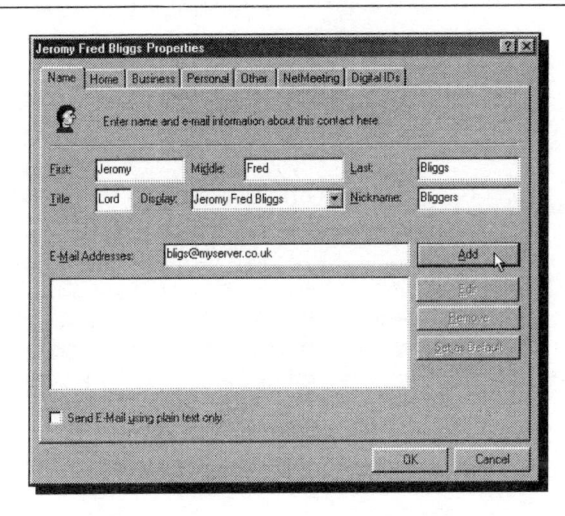

Address Book Help

We will leave it to you to find your way round this very comprehensive facility. Don't forget that it has its own Help system that you can use with the **Help**, **Contents and Index** menu command. An example section is shown open below.

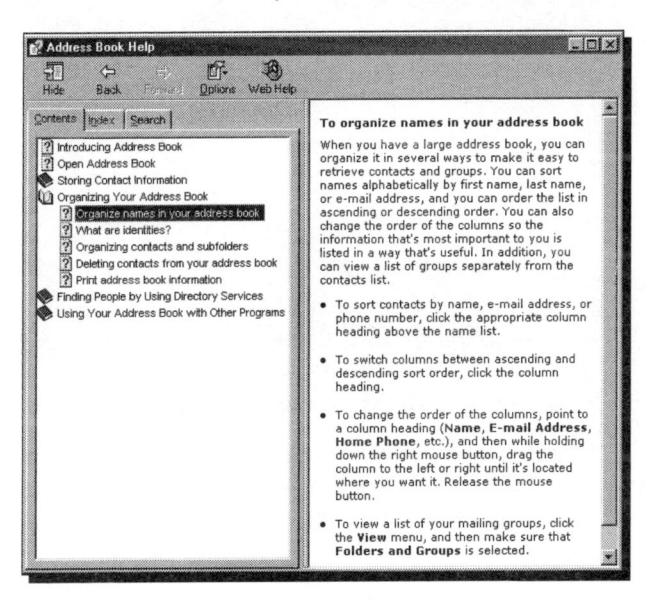

Using Message Rules

If you are ever in the situation of receiving e-mail messages from a source you do not want to hear from, you can use Message Rules to filter your incoming messages. Unwanted ones can be placed in your Deleted Items folder straight away. It can also be useful for sorting incoming messages and automatically routing them to their correct folders.

To open this feature, which is shown below, use the **Tools**, **Message Rules**, **Mail** menu command and select the criteria you want your incoming messages to be processed by.

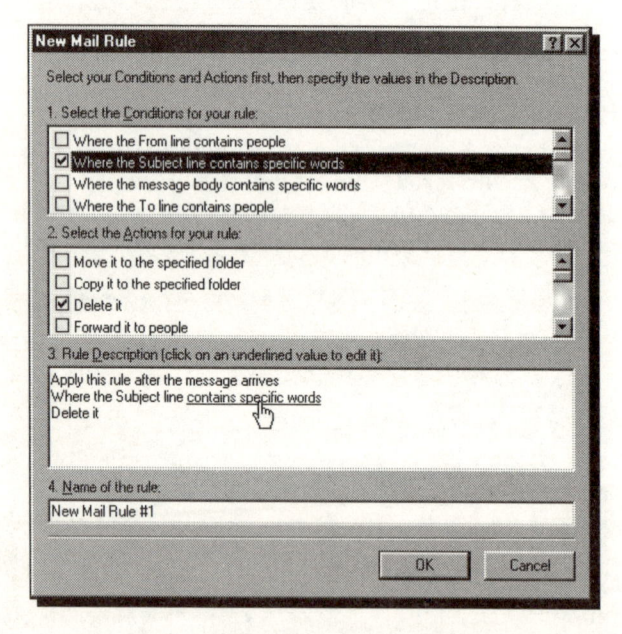

In box 1 above, you select the conditions for the new rule. In box 2 you control what actions are taken, and the new rule itself is automatically 'built' for you in box 3. If you use this feature much you will probably want to name each of your rules in box 4.

Some Other E-mail Features 8

In our example on the previous page, we have set to intercept and delete messages which contain certain words in their Subject Lines. To complete the rule we clicked on the 'contains specific words' link and filled in the following dialogue box.

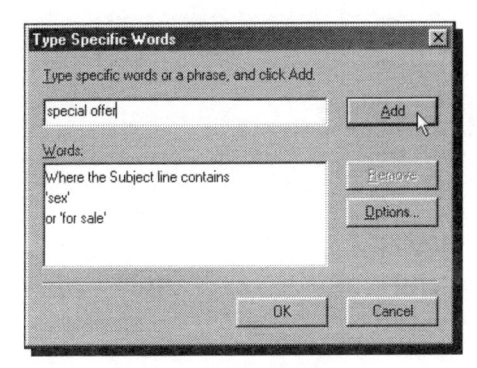

When finished clicking on **OK** twice opens the Message Rules box shown below.

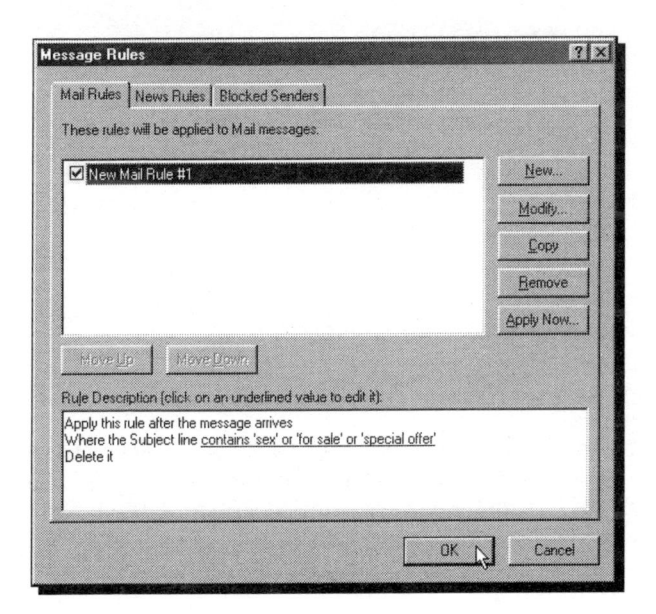

8   Some Other E-mail Features

In this box you can control your rules. You can set multiple rules for incoming messages and control the priority that messages are sorted in the list. The higher up a multiple list a condition is the higher will be its priority.

If an incoming message matches more than one rule, then it is sorted according to the first rule it matches in your list.

Blocked Senders List

With Outlook Express 5 there is a very easy way to prevent messages from a problem source ever disturbing your peace again. When you first receive such a message, select it in the Messages List and action the **Message**, **Block Sender** menu command, as we did in the example below.

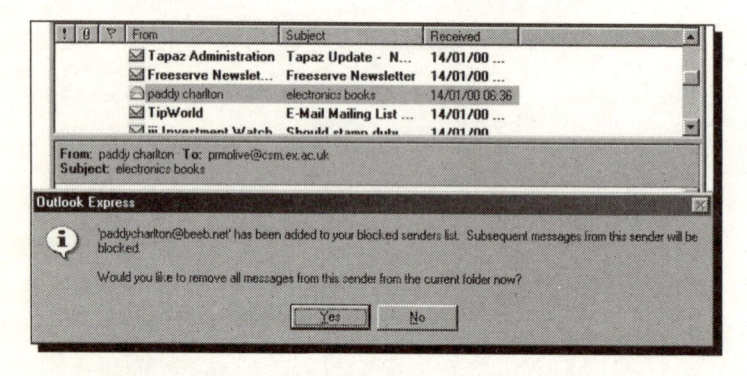

This can be a very powerful tool, be careful how you use it!

The **Message**, **Create Rule from Message** menu command is a quick way to start the New Rule process, as the details of the currently selected message are automatically placed in the New Mail Rule box for you.

People that send mass junk mailings often buy lists of e-mail addresses and once you are on a list you can be sure that your mailbox will never be empty again! With these tools at your disposal you should only ever receive 'junk mail' once from any particular source.

Some Other E-mail Features 8

Microsoft Hotmail

As we saw at the end of Chapter 2, if you don't have a mail account with an Internet Service Provider you can always use one of the free HTTP (Hypertext Transfer Protocol) services like Hotmail, where your messages are stored on a server. Using it you can access your e-mail from any computer with an Internet connection, anywhere in the world.

You have to be live to sign up with Hotmail, so you may have to do it from work, or a friend's PC, or a Cyber Cafe. From the Main Outlook Express window use the **Tools**, **New Account Signup** command and select **Hotmail** (with us it was the only option anyway), to open the following box.

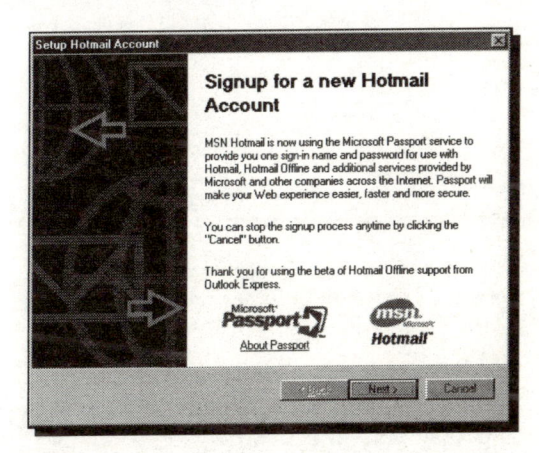

This was the first of eight boxes in our case. You have to complete each one before the **Next** button will let you proceed. None of them were particularly onerous, and after about only twenty minutes we were registered, as follows.

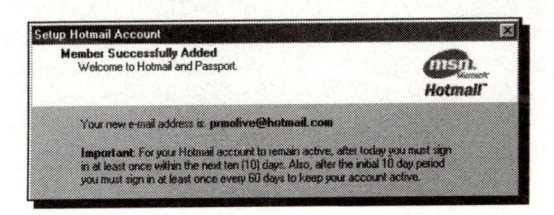

115

8 Some Other E-mail Features

Clicking the **Finish** button (not shown on our example) completes the procedure, and a new Folder icon should be added to the Folders List, as shown here.

The first time you click the new Hotmail icon it downloads several standard Hotmail folders for you to use.

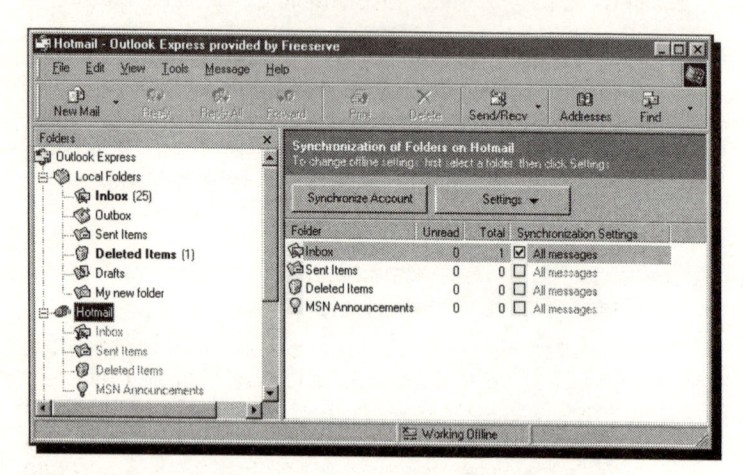

If you look carefully in the Folders List above, you can see that the entries in the Hotmail section are a lighter grey, this is because the folders are actually stored on a distant server, not on your PC.

Having a server-based account allows you to save time by downloading only your message headers so that you can choose which messages you want to later download and view in their entirety.

When you work 'offline', using the **File**, **Work Offline** menu command, you can read and respond to your e-mail messages just as you would when working online. The next time you go online, maybe by clicking the **Synchronize Account** button shown above, your server-based mail account will synchronise the mail on your computer with the server. During this process, the actions you performed in your account will be duplicated on the server.

Mailing Lists

When you start using e-mail you will probably want to receive lots of messages, but until your friends get active there is often a lull. This may be the time to join a mailing list.

Mailing lists are automatic mailing systems where a message sent to a list address is automatically sent on to all the other members of the list. The programs that manage this automatic mailing have names like Listserv, or Majordomo, which usually form part of the List address. Some of these lists are moderated and work much like journals, where submissions are accepted, sometimes edited, and then forwarded to subscribers. Others, however, have no constraints put on their contents! Although the quality and quantity vary from list to list, you can often find a wealth of free information in them.

To subscribe to a list, you need to know the name of the list and its address. Commands can vary between different lists, but they often follow the format given below. Note that there is a difference between the address to which you send postings, or messages, for the list, and the address you use for subscribing to it. Be sure to distinguish between these two addresses. One of the most common mistakes made by new Internet users is to send subscription requests to list addresses, which are then forwarded to all the members on the list. Please don't make this mistake, it can be annoying and time consuming for other list readers.

Finding a Suitable List

There are literally thousands of Mailing lists which you can join, covering almost every subject imaginable, from science, to art, to hobbies, and of course to any type of kinky sex. One of the biggest problems is finding the ones for you. Fortunately, there are several Web sites which give details of Mailing lists. A good one we have used, with lists grouped by topic should be found at:

http://wwwneosoft.com/internet/paml/subjects

Some Other E-mail Features

This will put you in direct contact with your selected lists, where you will get instructions on how to subscribe and proceed. Make sure you keep a copy of any instructions, you will need them in the future, if you want to unsubscribe, or change your subscription details.

Typical Subscription Commands

All of these commands go to the subscription address:

sub *listname* **First Last** To subscribe to *listname*, with your *First* and *Last* names given.

signoff *listname* To unsubscribe from a list.

set *listname* **nomail** To turn off mail from a list if you are going away.

set *listname* **mail** To turn the mail back on when you return.

Once you have mastered Mailing lists you need never have an empty mailbox again. In fact you may find them to be a little overpowering, but lists can be a wonderful source of up to date information.

Often Used E-mail Symbols

Once you start receiving messages from lists and other places around the globe, you may encounter some of the following acronyms, and symbols, which people often use to relieve the general boredom of life.

Acronyms

Btw	By the way
cu	See you (bye)
Faq	Frequently asked question
fyi	For your information
imho	In my humble opinion
imo	In my opinion
Rotfl	Rolling on the floor laughing
rtfm	Read the manual!
Ttyl	Talk to you later

Smileys

You tilt your head sideways to see them:

:-)	Smiling
:-D	Laughing
;-)	Winking
:-O	Surprise
:-(	Frowning, Sad
:-I	Indifferent
:-/	Perplexed
:-{)	Smiley with a moustache
8-)	Smiley with glasses
<:-|	Dunce
:-X	My lips are sealed
:->	Sarcastic

8 Some Other E-mail Features

If these appeal to you, you can get a more comprehensive selection from the *Unofficial Smiley Dictionary* reached at the following Web address:

http://www.eff.org/papers/eegtti/eeg_286.html#SEC287

9

News with Outlook Express 5

Discussion groups, or 'newsgroups', are a main feature of the Internet and are easily accessed with Outlook Express. They are often known as Usenet groups and consist of many thousands of separate news groups which let you actively take part in discussion on a vast number of topics. In fact almost any subject you could think of is covered, and the number of groups is growing larger all the time.

Outlook Express is a program you can use for viewing, and posting (or mailing), messages to these Usenet groups. Unlike e-mail, which is usually 'one-to-one', newsgroups could be said to be 'one-to-many'.

How Usenet Works

Usenet messages are shipped around the world, from host system to host system, using one of several available protocols, that you don't need to bother too much about. Your host server stores all of its Usenet messages in one place, which everybody with an account on the system can access, if they want. That way, no matter how many people actually read a given message, each host has to store only one copy of it. The host systems contact each other regularly and bring themselves up to date with the latest Usenet messages, sometimes this happens thousands of times a day.

Usenet is huge. We once saw it quoted that every day Usenet users transmit over 60 million characters into the system. Some of this information has to be of use! In fact there are so many active groups now, it is unlikely that your server will handle more than a fraction of them. This can be frustrating, if you keep seeing references to a group that you cannot access through your server.

Usenet Newsgroups

The basic building block of Usenet as we have seen is the newsgroup, which is a collection of messages with a related theme. These are arranged in a particular hierarchy that originated in the early 80s. Newsgroup names start with one of a series of broad topic names. For example, newsgroups beginning with '**sci**' should have scientific and engineering content. These broad topics are followed by a series of more specific topic names. '**sci.engr**' groups, for example, are limited to discussion about engineering subjects, and '**sci.engr.mining**' would be a group dedicated to very specific discussion on mining engineering topics.

There are many national and regional groups, including **uk**, but some of the main topic headers are:

alt	Controversial, sexual, and unusual topics; not always carried by servers.
bionet	Research biology.
bit.listserv	Conferences originating as Bitnet mailing lists.
biz	Business.
comp	Computers and related subjects.
misc	Discussions that don't fit anywhere else.
news	News about Usenet and its groups.
rec	Hobbies, games and recreation.
sci	Science and engineering, other than research biology.
soc	Social groups, often ethnically related.
talk	Politics and related topics.

With such an almost unlimited choice, you should very soon be able to subscribe to your own unique reading list of newsgroups. Subscribing does not mean you have to pay something, but means that when you enter News you will only see the groups in which you are most interested, and won't have to search through all of the others every time.

Starting to Read News

Initially you can start the News process from the opening window of Outlook Express 5, by clicking the 'Subscribe to Newsgroups' link as shown below.

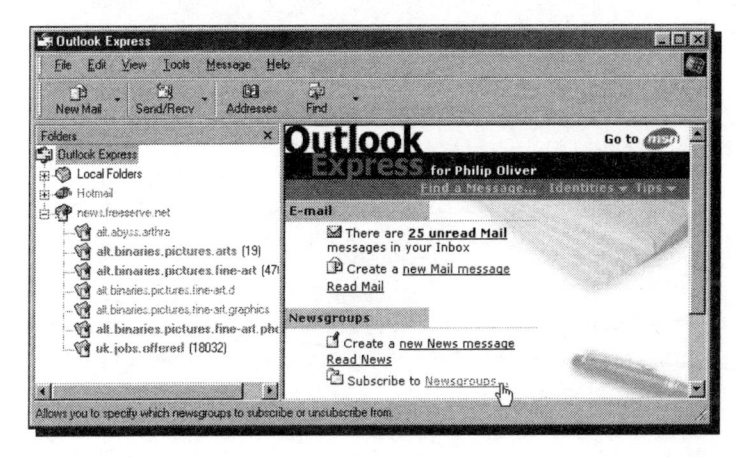

When first used, this opens the Internet Connection Wizard for you to complete your details. Once this has been completed and you have subscribed to one, or more, newsgroups, you simply click on a newsgroup folder in the Folders List to access that newsgroup. Our example above shows seven newsgroups and one news server in the list.

Internet News Configuration

Before you can access the Usenet groups you must make sure that your details and those of your news server are entered into the Internet Connection Wizard. If necessary, you can open this from the **Tools**, **Accounts**, **News** settings box by clicking the **Add** button and then selecting **News**.

Complete the details in the dialogue boxes as they are presented, entering the server name in the **News (NNTP) server** field, as shown here.

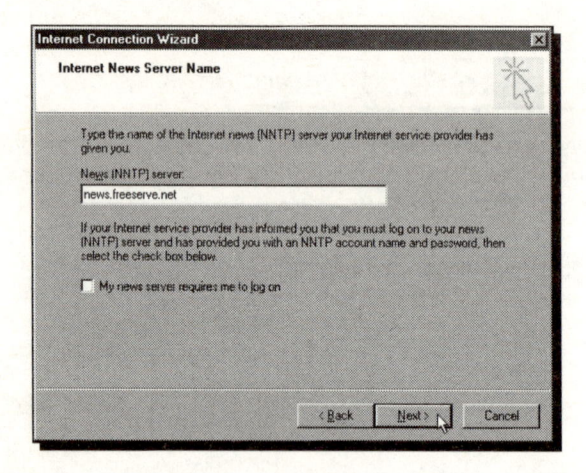

If this is a closed, or members-only type server, then complete the log-on details which you should have been given. Otherwise keep clicking **Next** until finally the program starts downloading the server groups. Be warned the whole procedure can take well over half an hour.

As can be seen in many of our examples, we use Freeserve as one of our Internet Service Providers. This service is free and available to anyone that registers, so you should have no problem following our examples if you want to. Freeserve's News service has about 35,000 newsgroups, which is nowhere near complete. To get 'all' of the groups, especially the more exciting 'alt' ones, you would probably have to register with one of the remaining pay services. Hence the saying 'You get what you pays for'.

There are also hundreds of open news servers on the Internet that allow you to connect to them without a password. You should be able to find lists of them by searching for 'open news servers' with one of the search engines. Open news servers do not often stay permanently available though.

News with Outlook Express

The Newsgroup Subscriptions Window

The initial set-up procedure finishes by downloading a list of all the groups available on the news server. As there are well over 35,000 available to some servers this can take quite a while. When this is done, a window similar to ours below opens and you can see what newsgroups are available to you. If you are subscribed to more than one server, the **Newsgroups** pane lists the groups available from the server selected in the **Account(s)** pane.

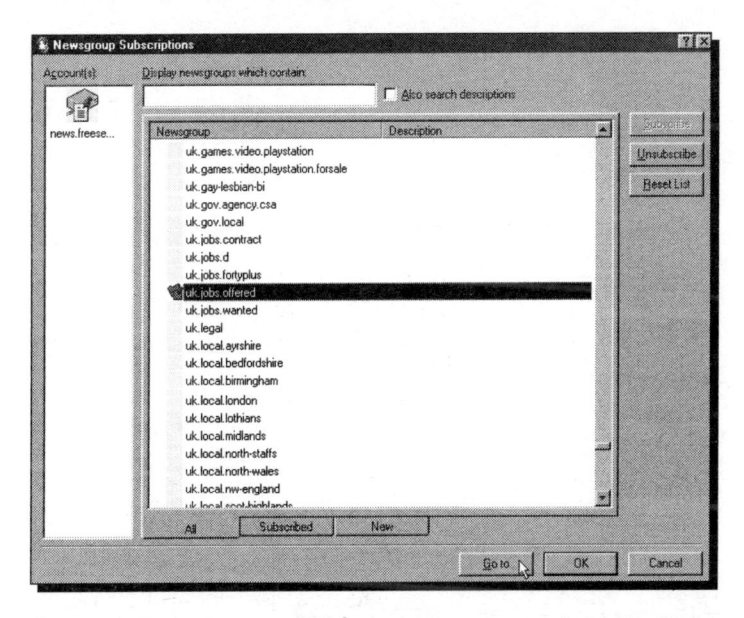

If you scroll down through the list of groups, almost at the bottom you should find some that start with **uk**. In our example, we selected **uk.jobs.offered** and clicked the **Go to** button, which is an easy way to have a look at the contents of a group. An easier way would have been to type 'uk.jobs' into the **Display newsgroups which contain** field. Only the seven that matched this criterion would then have displayed.

A one-line header (for each of the first 300 of the 18,032 messages contained in the group that day), was loaded into

9 News with Outlook Express

the Message Header pane, as shown below. Not too much unemployment in the computer industry these days!

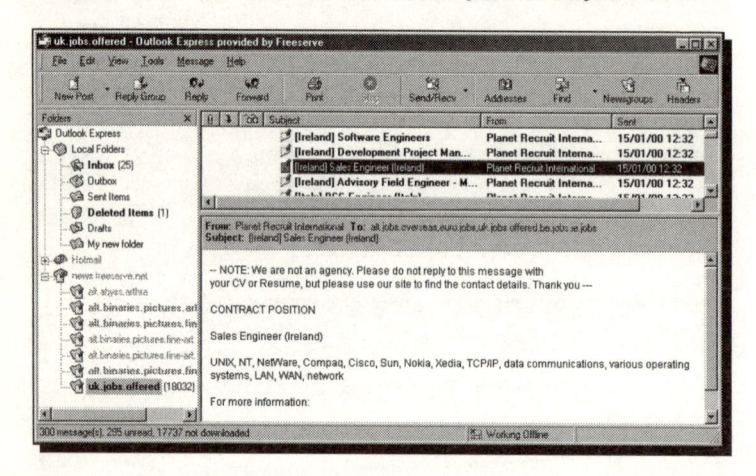

As soon as one of these headers is selected, the message itself appears in the Preview pane below it. This can take a few moments, don't forget it has to be downloaded over the network from your server.

Subscribing to a Group

If you think a group looks interesting and would be useful in the future, you should subscribe to it. To do this, re-open the Newsgroup Subscriptions window by clicking the Newsgroups Toolbar button, highlight the group and click the **Subscribe** button. A newspaper icon is placed alongside the group name in the listing. To remove a group from your subscribed list, you simply select it and click the **Unsubscribe** button.

Once you have selected all the groups you regularly want to keep tabs on, click the **Subscribed** tab button at the bottom of the list. In the future, each time you open the Newsgroups window, it will only display your chosen list. At any time while this window is open you can click **All** to see a complete listing again, or **New** to see any new groups.

The News Window

The News window, shown on the facing page, is almost the same as the Main e-mail window. It contains three panes, a Folders List, a Message Header List, and a Preview pane.

Clicking on a Newsgroup in the Folders List, displays a listing of that group's current headers in the Message Header List, which by default has seven columns:

📎	Message has file(s) attached.
⬇	Message is marked for offline viewing.
👓	Watch/ignore this conversation.
Subject	Shows the subject line of the message.
From	Gives the 'name' of the sender of the news message.
Sent	States the date and time the message was posted to the group.
Size	Gives the size of the file in KB.

You can sort messages by any of these columns and in ascending or descending order, by clicking in the column header. You can also add, remove, or rearrange the columns, and sort them, with the **View**, **Columns** menu command.

Clicking on a message header, when you are on-line, downloads and displays the message body text in the Preview pane.

The News Toolbar

New Post — Opens a New Message window for creating a new e-mail message, with the To: field blank.

Reply Group — Opens the New Message window for sending a message to be posted in the currently selected newsgroup.

Reply — Opens the New Message window for replying privately to the sender of the current news message, with the To: field pre-addressed to the original sender.

Forward — Opens the New Message window for forwarding the current news message. The To: field is blank. The original Subject field is prefixed with Fw:.

Print — Prints the current message.

Stop — Stops the current downloading operation. This option is only available when the download Status Indicator in the top right corner of the window is rotating.

Send/Recv — Attempts to make a dial-up connection and downloads selected messages or headers, as well as updating any e-mail folders and sending any waiting messages.

Addresses — Opens the Outlook Express Address Book.

Find — Lets you search for messages, text, or for people's e-mail details.

Newsgroups — Opens the Newsgroup Subscriptions window in which you select which news server to use and the groups subscribed to.

Headers — Downloads new headers for the selected group from the server, in batches of 300.

The Read Message Window

Double-clicking on a message header in the News window, opens a Read Message window with the message in it, as shown below.

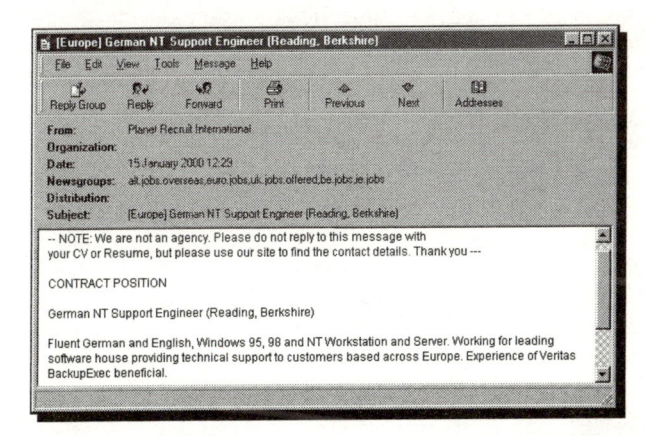

This window has its own menu and Toolbar, and moving the mouse pointer over a Toolbar button shows what the button's action will be. Apart from the three icons described below, this window is very much the same as the e-mail Read Message window described in an earlier chapter.

Replying to Messages

As long as you have chosen to make Outlook Express your default news reader in the **Tools**, **Options**, **General** settings box, the News window Toolbar icons will use the Mail facilities to easily send messages of three different types.

The **Reply to Group** icon addresses your message to the current newsgroup for all to read.

The **Reply to Sender** icon addresses an e-mail message to the individual who posted the current news message.

News with Outlook Express

The **Forward** icon prepares an e-mail with a copy of the current message, for you to address and complete.

Be very careful not to mix these up, the result could be embarrassing if you post a very personal message to the whole group, for maybe millions of people to read!

Postings Containing Pictures

If you have time to explore the many thousands of **alt** groups, you will find that a lot of them contain messages with picture files attached that are (or should be) relevant to the group name. Our example below shows one being downloaded from a group that does not normally need censoring, but be warned, many of them do these days! You never really know what you will find in them.

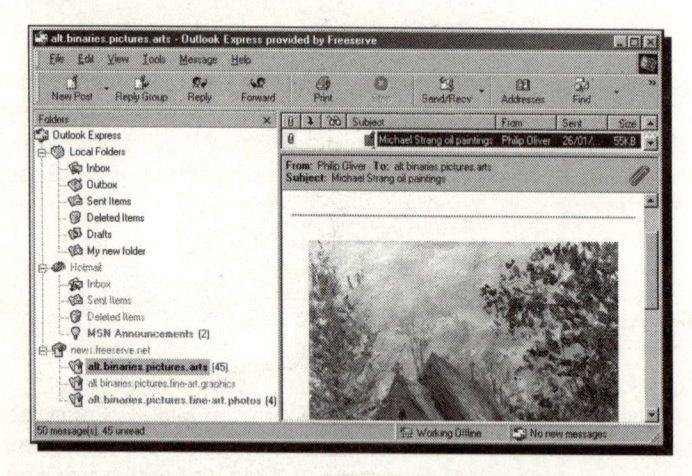

Clicking a message in the Header Pane will, as long as you are connected, download the message body in the Preview pane, and you will be able to view any graphics in the message, as shown above. When the image file has been completely downloaded, you can use the **File**, **Save Attachments** command to save any images in it to your hard disc.

Usually a paper clip icon is placed on the title bar of the Preview pane, as with e-mail attachments. Clicking this icon will show the name of the attached file and give you the option to **Save Attachments**.

The same message with the whole example of excellent English contemporary art is shown above, but this time opened in its own Read Message window, by double-clicking the message header. The image attachment is shown in its own **Attach** box below the message headers.

To view, or run other message attachments, double-click their icons. As before, to save a file attachment, use the **File**, **Save Attachments** menu command, or right-click the attachment and select the **Save Picture As** option.

Threaded Messages

When a message is placed on a newsgroup, often someone replies and then a 'thread' or 'conversation' is formed.

> **News message icons**
> The following icons indicate whether a conversation (a topic and all of its responses) is expanded or collapsed, and whether messages and headers are marked as read or unread.
>
> | This icon | Indicates this |
> |---|---|
> | ⊞ | This level of the conversation is collapsed. Click the icon to show all the responses (expand the conversation). |
> | ⊟ | This level of the conversation is expanded. Click the icon to hide all the responses (collapse the conversation). |
> | | The message has not been not opened. The heading appears in bold type. |
> | | The message header has been marked read. |
> | | The message has been marked read, and is stored in a message file on your computer. |
> | | The message has not been marked as read, and the header and body are stored in a message file on your computer. |
> | | The message is no longer available on the server. |
> | | The news message is marked to be downloaded. |
> | | The news message and all conversations are marked to be downloaded. |
> | | The individual news message (without conversations) is marked to be downloaded. |
> | | The news message has been replied to. |
> | | The news message has been forwarded. |
> | ✻ | The newsgroup is new on the server. |
> | | The message is in progress in the Drafts folder. |
> | ⚑ | The message is flagged. |
> | | The conversation is watched. |
> | ⊘ | The conversation is ignored. |

The edited News Help window above shows how you can recognise the status of any news messages in the Message Header list of a News window. Outlook Express messages are not threaded by default, but you can change this by checking the **Automatically expand grouped messages** option in the **Tools**, **Options**, **Read** settings sheet. Message replies would then always be placed with the original messages.

If you want the message list to display only the original message in a thread (conversation), select the first message, and then use the **View**, **Collapse** menu command, or click the minus (-) sign next to the original message.

Offline Viewing

If, like most of us, you are usually busy and don't have time to wait for long newsgroup messages to be downloaded, you can synchronise your accounts, or set up a batch download process, and view selected headers or whole messages off-line later on.

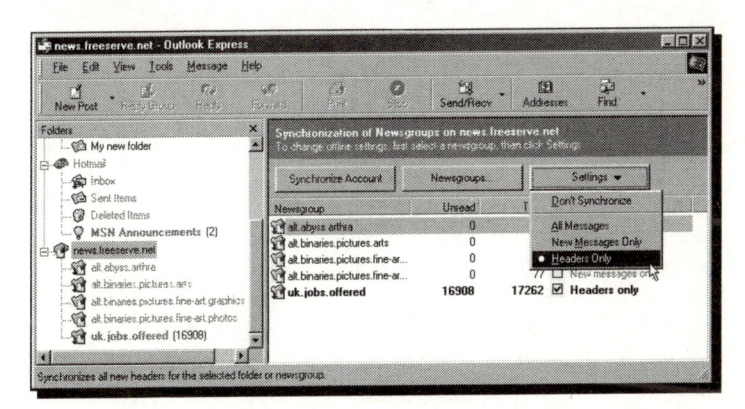

In the Main window in Offline mode, select one or more newsgroups you subscribe to whose messages you want to read offline. Click the **Settings** button, and then select the option you want from the drop-down menu, as shown above. This marks the group with what you want transferred from the server to your computer during synchronisation.

All Messages — Download all messages on the server to your computer.

New Messages Only — Download only messages that are new to the server since you last synchronised.

Headers Only — Download only headers with details of message subject, author, date, and size.

Whenever you want to transfer the messages or headers to your computer from the server, click the **Synchronize Account** button and go and make a cup of coffee.

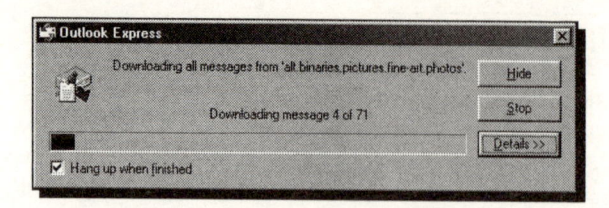

A downloading box, similar to the one above, will show you how the download process is going. You can click the **Details** button to see more information about what is happening. If you are using a modem connection, you should definitely check the **Hang up when finished** option. Your phone bill will almost certainly be big enough already!

After you download messages for off-line reading and have disconnected from the Internet, you can return to the News Window and the message header icons, shown on Page 132, will show the status of any saved, or cached, headers or messages. Clicking the **View**, **Current View**, **Show Downloaded Messages** menu command, will display only the downloaded messages for you to read. Have fun.

Newsgroup Caches

Each newsgroup you subscribe to has its own cache file on your computer and everything you download from that group, either manually or for off-line viewing, is saved in this cache. When you select to view an item that is stored in a cache it is 'instantly' displayed, as it does not have to be downloaded. This is all very well, but if you are not careful you can fill your hard disc up with material you don't even know you are keeping.

Controlling the Caches

The **Tools**, **Options**, **Maintenance** settings sheet gives you control of the size of all your cached message files when you click the **Clean Up Now** button.

News with Outlook Express 9

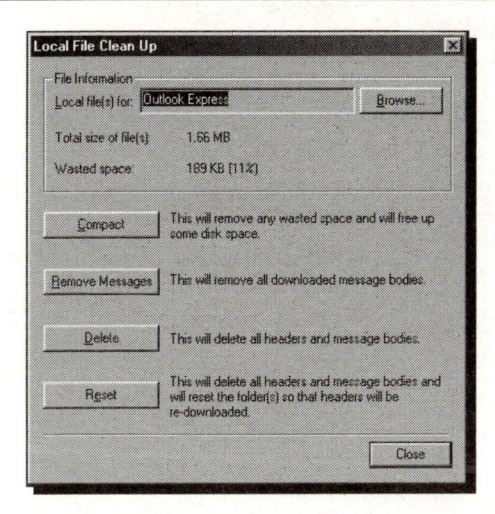

Here you can manually compact, delete, or remove messages from all or specific message files, newsgroups, or servers, including Hotmail. You access all these 'local' files on your PC by clicking the **Browse** button.

This clean-up procedure is usually known as 'purging'. Some of these 'manual clean up' options are also available from the News menu with the **File**, **Folder** command.

Purging unused, old, or large newsgroups can increase your free hard disc space enormously. Most news servers remove old messages and headers on a regular basis, sometimes even weekly. The next time you connect to a newsgroup you've purged, your cache is rebuilt with just the current messages and headers from the server.

On Your Own

You should, by now, have enough basic knowledge to happily venture forth into the unknown.

Good luck, but please remember that there are millions of other newsgroup readers, and you never know where, or who, they are. Please watch what you say, or include, in your postings, there is enough rubbish there already.

10

Behaviour on the Internet

As we saw in the first chapter, the Internet has grown up without any real control. It has grown, just like Topsy, but some of the behaviour you see there is not always quite as nice. We will not talk about pornography, or worse. If that is what you want, it is almost certainly there to be found (as in most major cities of the world), but increasingly it is hidden behind closed doors. Most really dubious Web sites require membership and payment, but the Usenet groups are still a problem. If you have children that use your computer to surf the Web, Internet Explorer has a security feature to help enable you to control what they are exposed to, this is briefly discussed at the end of the chapter.

We will very briefly mention some of the more dubious behaviour patterns you may encounter on your way round the Internet, especially in the newsgroups, and to a lesser extent the mailing lists.

Internet Flames

A flame is a particularly nasty, personal attack on somebody for something he, or she, has written in a posting. Newsgroups are notorious for flaming (burning people up). This can sometimes lead to long and drawn-out discussions on what really are stupid matters. These 'flame wars' can sometimes be fun to watch at first, but quickly grow boring, and become a general waste of everyone's time and mail space.

But, be warned, once you start posting to groups you may well upset someone, without even meaning to. If they are vicious, you may get flamed.

Spam, Spam, Bacon and Spam

Spamming, on the Internet, is the practice of sending a message to a very large number of people, newsgroups and mailing lists. It is named after the Monty Python sketch, where you could have what you liked in the restaurant as long as it had spam with it. A spammer gives you little choice, you have to download his posting, but you don't have to read it.

It will not be long before you encounter this 'problem' in some form, or other. Often a product, service, or a get rich quick scheme is being offered. We tend to ignore them and hope they will go away.

Other Usenet Types

There are a number of other Usenet types you'll soon come to recognise, and love:

Ones that think their topic of interest should be forced on everyone else as frequently as possible. Often posting dozens of messages to unrelated groups, sometimes with ethnic contents.

Ones that take pages of message to get nowhere. This often includes excessive quoting by including the entire message in their reply, rather than deleting the irrelevant portions.

Ones who enjoy insulting others and post nasty, or even obscene, messages in unrelated newsgroups.

Ones who include enormous signatures at the end of their postings, often including enormous text graphics. These are harmless, but can be annoying.

Some Internet Etiquette

Often called 'netiquette' the following list, we once found[1], although somewhat stilted makes good reading and should help you avoid upsetting too many people on the Net:

1 DON'T include the entire contents of a previous posting in your reply.

DO cut mercilessly. Leave just enough to indicate what you're responding to. NEVER include mail headers except maybe the 'From:' line. If you can't figure out how to delete lines in your mailer software, paraphrase or re-type the quoted material.

2 DON'T reply to a point in a message without quoting or paraphrasing what you're responding to.

DO quote (briefly) or paraphrase. If the original 'Subject:' line was 'Big dogs' make sure yours says 'Re: Big dogs'. Some REPLY functions do this automatically. By net convention, included lines are preceded by '>' (greater-than signs).

3 DON'T send lines longer than 70 characters. This is a kindness to folks with terminal-based mail editors. Some mail gateways truncate extra characters turning your deathless prose into gibberish.

Some mail editor tools only SEEM to insert line breaks for you, but actually don't, so that every paragraph is one immense line. Learn what your mail editor does.

4 DON'T SEND A MESSAGE IN ALL CAPS. CAPITALISED MESSAGES ARE HARDER TO READ THAN LOWER CASE OR MIXED CASE.

---

[1] Patrick Crispen's Internet Roadmap

10   Behaviour on the Internet

DO use normal capitalisation. Separate your paragraphs with blank lines. Make your message inviting to your potential readers.

5   DON'T betray confidences. It is all too easy to quote a personal message and regret it.

DO read the 'To:' and 'Cc:' lines in your message before you send it. Are you SURE you want the mail to go there?

6   DON'T make statements which can be interpreted as official positions of your organisation, or of offers to do business.

DO treat every post as though you were sending a copy to your boss, your minister, and your worst enemy.

7   DON'T rely on the ability of your readers to tell the difference between serious statements and satire, or sarcasm. It's hard to write funny. It's even harder to write satire.

DO remember that no one can hear your tone of voice. Use smileys, like:

:-) or **:->**

turn your head anti-clockwise to see the smile.

You can also use capitals for emphasis, or use Net conventions for italics and underlines as in: "You said the guitar solo on "Comfortably Numb" from Pink Floyd's, The Wall, was *lame*? Are you OUT OF YOUR MIND???!!!"

8   DON'T send a message that says nothing but "Me, too", or something equally as trivial. This is most annoying when combined with (1) or (2) above.

Censoring your Web Browser

Internet Explorer 5 allows you to control what Web sites your children can access. This feature is located on the **Tools**, **Internet Options**, **Content** settings sheet shown here.

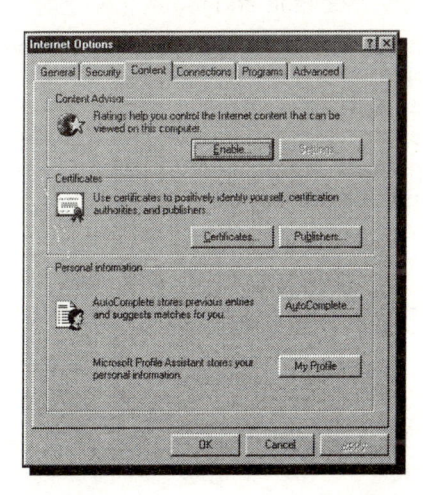

Clicking the **Enable** button opens the Content Adviser control window, shown below. This has four sliders to allow you to set the degree of language, nudity, sex and violence you want your children (or other users) to be exposed to.

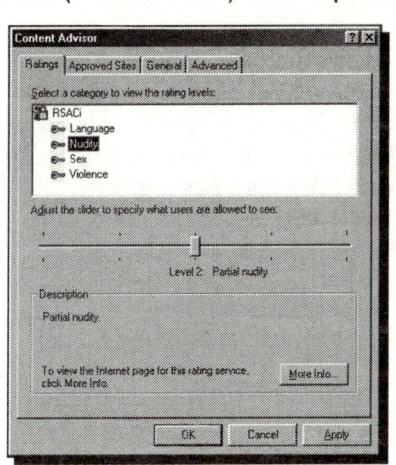

This facility depends on Web sites having a rating system 'attached to them'. The Content Adviser then filters out unsuitable sites and prohibits access to them. The default site rating service is provided by the Recreational Software Advisory Council (RSAC). There is the facility to select others in the **Advanced** tab section.

By default, if a Web site does not have a rating your users will not be able to access it. They will be presented with a blacked out screen if they try. You can alter this, however, in the **General** tab section, by checking the **Users can see sites that have no rating** option. Also in this section you can use the **Change Password** feature.

When you have made all the settings you want, press **OK** enough times to close the Content Adviser. You will be asked to establish a password, but please don't forget it or you will find yourself re-installing Explorer in the future! You have now censored your computer, probably for the first time!

To cancel, or change, your security settings in the future, open the **Tools**, **Internet Options**, **Content** sheet and click the **Disable** button. You will need your password to access the Content Adviser.

This measure could also be usefully used by organisations to limit their personnel to specific sites on the Internet. This would not be a popular measure, but would almost certainly reduce the amount of wasted time.

Still a Feature for the Future

We feel this feature is a commendable attempt by Microsoft to make surfing the Web a safer place for your children, but it does depend on all the 'non-exotic' sites getting rated. At the moment this is anything but the case.

11

Glossary of Terms

ActiveX	A set of technologies that enables software components to interact with one another in a networked environment, regardless of the language in which the components were created.
Add-in	A mini-program which runs in conjunction with another and enhances its functionality.
Address	A unique number or name that identifies a specific computer or user on a network.
Anonymous FTP	Anonymous FTP allows you to connect to a remote computer and transfer public files back to your local computer without the need to have a user ID and password.
Application	Software (program) designed to carry out certain activity, such as word processing, or data management.
Applet	A program that can be downloaded over a network and launched on the user's computer.
Archie	Archie is an Internet service that allows you to locate files that can be downloaded via FTP.

11 Glossary of Terms

ASP	Active Server Page. File format used for dynamic Web pages that get their data from a server based database.
Association	An identification of a filename extension to a program. This lets Windows open the program when its files are selected.
ASCII	A binary code representation of a character set. The name stands for 'American Standard Code for Information Interchange'.
Authoring	The process of creating web documents or software.
AVI	Audio Video Interleaved. A Windows multimedia file format for sound and moving pictures.
Backbone	The main transmission lines of the Internet, running at over 45Mbps.
Backup	To make a back-up copy of a file or a disc for safekeeping.
Bandwidth	The range of transmission frequencies a network can use. The greater the bandwidth the more information that can be transferred over a network.
Banner	An advertising graphic shown on a Web page.
BASIC	Beginner's All-purpose Symbolic Instruction Code - a high-level programming language.
BBS	Bulletin Board System, a computer equipped with software and telecoms links that allow it to act as an information host for remote computer systems.

Beta test	A test of software that is still under development, by people actually using the software.
BinHex	A file conversion format that converts binary files to ASCII text files.
Bitmap	A technique for managing the image displayed on a computer screen.
Bookmark	A marker inserted at a specific point in a document to which the user may wish to return for later reference.
Bound control	A control on a database form, report or data access page that is tied to a field in an underlying table or query.
Browse	A button in some Windows dialogue boxes that lets you view a list of files and folders before you make a selection.
Browser	A program, like the Internet Explorer, that lets you view Web pages.
Bug	An error in coding or logic that causes a program to malfunction.
Button	A graphic element in a dialogue box or toolbar that performs a specified function.
Cache	An area of memory, or disc space, reserved for data, which speeds up downloading.
Card	A removable printed-circuit board that is plugged into a computer expansion slot.
CD-ROM	Compact Disc - Read Only Memory; an optical disc which information may be read from but not written to.

11　Glossary of Terms

CGI	Common Gateway Interface - a convention for servers to communicate with local applications and allow users to provide information to scripts attached to web pages, usually through forms.
Cgi-bin	The most common name of a directory on a web server in which CGI programs are stored.
Chart	A graphical view of data that is used to visually display trends, patterns, and comparisons.
Click	To press and release a mouse button once without moving the mouse.
Client	A computer that has access to services over a computer network. The computer providing the services is a server.
Client application	A Windows application that can accept linked, or embedded, objects.
Clipboard	A temporary storage area of memory, where text and graphics are stored with the Windows cut and copy actions.
Command	An instruction given to a computer to carry out a particular action.
Compressed file	One that is compacted to save server space and reduce transfer times. Typical file extensions for compressed files include .zip (DOS/Windows) and .tar (UNIX).
Configuration	A general purpose term referring to the way you have your computer set up.

Glossary of Terms

Controls	Objects on a form, report, or data access page that display data, perform actions, or are used for decoration.
Cookies	Files stored on your hard drive by your Web browser that hold information for it to use.
CPU	The Central Processing Unit; the main chip that executes all instructions entered into a computer.
Cyberspace	Originated by William Gibson in his novel 'Neuromancer', now used to describe the Internet and the other computer networks.
Data access page	A Web page, created by Access, that has a connection to a database; you can view, add, edit, and manipulate the data in this page.
Database	A collection of data related to a particular topic or purpose.
DBMS	Database management system - A software interface between the database and the user.
Dial-up Connection	A popular form of Net connection for the home user, over standard telephone lines.
Direct Connection	A permanent connection between your computer system and the Internet.
Default	The command, device or option automatically chosen.
Desktop	The Windows screen working background, on which you place icons, folders, etc.

11 Glossary of Terms

Device driver
: A special file that must be loaded into memory for Windows to be able to address a specific procedure or hardware device.

Device name
: A logical name used by DOS to identify a device, such as LPT1 or COM1 for the parallel or serial printer.

Dialogue box
: A window displayed on the screen to allow the user to enter information.

Directory
: An area on disc where information relating to a group of files is kept. Also known as a folder.

Disc
: A device on which you can store programs and data.

Disconnect
: To detach a drive, port or computer from a shared device, or to break an Internet connection.

Document
: A file produced by an application program. When used in reference to the Web, a document is any file containing text, media or hyperlinks that can be transferred from an HTTP server to a browser.

Domain
: A group of devices, servers and computers on a network.

Domain Name
: The name of an Internet site, for example www.michaelstrang.com, which allows you to reference Internet sites without knowing their true numerical address.

DOS
: Disc Operating System. A collection of small specialised programs that allow interaction between user and computer.

Glossary of Terms 11

Double-click	To quickly press and release a mouse button twice.
Download	To transfer to your computer a file, or data, from another computer.
DPI	Dots Per Inch - a resolution standard for laser printers.
Drag	To move an object on the screen by pressing and holding down the left mouse button while moving the mouse.
Drive name	The letter followed by a colon which identifies a floppy or hard disc drive.
EISA	Extended Industry Standard Architecture, for construction of PCs with the Intel 32-bit micro-processor.
Embedded object	Information in a document that is 'copied' from its source application. Selecting the object opens the creating application from within the document.
Engine	Software used by search services.
E-mail	Electronic Mail - A system that allows computer users to send and receive messages electronically.
Ethernet	A very common method of networking computers in a LAN.
FAQ	Frequently Asked Questions - A common feature on the Internet, FAQs are files of answers to commonly asked questions.
FAT	The File Allocation Table. An area on disc where information is kept on which part of the disc a file is located.

149

11 Glossary of Terms

File extension	The suffix following the period in a filename. Windows uses this to identify the source application program. For example .mdb indicates an Access file.
Filename	The name given to a file. In Windows 95 and above this can be up to 256 characters long.
Filter	A set of criteria that is applied to data to show a subset of the data.
Firewall	Security measures designed to protect a networked system from unauthorised access.
Floppy disc	A removable disc on which information can be stored magnetically.
Folder	An area used to store a group of files, usually with a common link.
Font	A graphic design representing a set of characters, numbers and symbols.
Freeware	Software that is available for downloading and unlimited use without charge.
FTP	File Transfer Protocol. The procedure for connecting to a remote computer and transferring files.
Function key	One of the series of 10 or 12 keys marked with the letter F and a numeral, used for specific operations.
Gateway	A computer system that allows otherwise incompatible networks to communicate with each other.

Glossary of Terms

GIF	Graphics Interchange Format, a common standard for images on the Web.
Graphic	A picture or illustration, also called an image. Formats include GIF, JPEG, BMP, PCX, and TIFF.
Graphics card	A device that controls the display on the monitor and other allied functions.
GUI	A Graphic User Interface, such as Windows 98, the software front-end meant to provide an attractive and easy to use interface.
Hard copy	Output on paper.
Hard disc	A device built into the computer for holding programs and data.
Hardware	The equipment that makes up a computer system, excluding the programs or software.
Help	A Windows system that gives you instructions and additional information on using a program.
Helper application	A program allowing you to view multimedia files that your web browser cannot handle internally.
Hit	A single request from a web browser for a single item from a web server.
Home page	The document displayed when you first open your Web browser, or the first document you come to at a Web site.
Host	Computer connected directly to the Internet that provides services to other local and/or remote computers.

11 Glossary of Terms

Hotlist	A list of frequently used Web locations and URL addresses.
Host	A computer acting as an information or communications server.
HTML	HyperText Markup Language, the format used in documents on the Web.
HTML editor	Authoring tool which assists with the creation of HTML pages.
HTTP	HyperText Transport Protocol, the system used to link and transfer hypertext documents on the Web.
Hyperlink	A segment of text, or an image, that refers to another document on the Web, an Intranet or your PC.
Hypermedia	Hypertext extended to include linked multimedia.
Hypertext	A system that allows documents to be cross-linked so that the reader can explore related links, or documents, by clicking on a highlighted symbol.
Icon	A small graphic image that represents a function or object. Clicking on an icon produces an action.
Image	See graphic.
Insertion point	A flashing bar that shows where typed text will be entered into a document.
Interface	A device that allows you to connect a computer to its peripherals.
Internet	The global system of computer networks.

Glossary of Terms

Intranet	A private network inside an organisation using the same kind of software as the Internet.
ISA	Industry Standard Architecture; a standard for internal connections in PCs.
ISDN	Integrated Services Digital Network, a telecom standard using digital transmission technology to support voice, video and data communications applications over regular telephone lines.
IP	Internet Protocol - The rules that provide basic Internet functions.
IP Address	Internet Protocol Address - every computer on the Internet has a unique identifying number.
ISP	Internet Service Provider - A company that offers access to the Internet.
Java	An object-oriented programming language created by Sun Microsystems for developing applications and applets that are capable of running on any computer, regardless of the operating system.
JPEG /JPG	Joint Photographic Experts Group, a popular cross-platform format for image files. JPEG is best suited for true colour original images.
Kilobyte	(KB); 1024 bytes of information or storage space.
LAN	Local Area Network - High-speed, privately-owned network covering a

11 Glossary of Terms

	limited geographical area, such as an office or a building.
Laptop	A portable computer small enough to sit on your lap.
LCD	Liquid Crystal Display.
Links	The hypertext connections between Web pages.
Local	A resource that is located on your computer, not linked to it over a network.
Location	An Internet address.
Log on	To gain access to a network.
MCI	Media Control Interface - a standard for files and multimedia devices.
Megabyte	(MB); 1024 kilobytes of information or storage space.
Megahertz	(MHz); Speed of processor in millions of cycles per second.
Memory	Part of computer consisting of storage elements organised into addressable locations that can hold data and instructions.
Menu	A list of available options in an application.
Menu bar	The horizontal bar that lists the names of menus.
MIDI	Musical Instrument Digital Interface - enables devices to transmit and receive sound and music messages.
MIME	Multipurpose Internet Mail Extensions, a messaging standard that allows Internet users to exchange

Glossary of Terms

	e-mail messages enhanced with graphics, video and voice.
MIPS	Million Instructions Per Second; measures speed of a system.
Modem	Short for Modulator-demodulator devices. An electronic device that lets computers communicate electronically.
Monitor	The display device connected to your PC, also called a screen.
Mouse	A device used to manipulate a pointer around your display and activate processes by pressing buttons.
MPEG	Motion Picture Experts Group - a video file format offering excellent quality in a relatively small file.
MS-DOS	Microsoft's implementation of the Disc Operating System for PCs.
Multimedia	The use of photographs, music and sound and movie images in a presentation.
Multi-tasking	Performing more than one operation at the same time.
Network	Two or more computers connected together to share resources.
Network server	Central computer which stores files for several linked computers.
Node	Any single computer connected to a network.
ODBC	Open DataBase Connectivity - A standard protocol for accessing information in a SQL database server.

11 Glossary of Terms

OLE	Object Linking and Embedding - A technology for transferring and sharing information among software applications.
Online	Having access to the Internet.
On-line Service	Services such as America On-line and CompuServe that provide content to subscribers and usually connections to the Internet.
Operating system	Software that runs a computer.
Page	An HTML document, or Web site.
Password	A unique character string used to gain access to a network, program, or mailbox.
PATH	The location of a file in the directory tree.
Peripheral	Any device attached to a PC.
Perl	A popular language for programming CGI applications.
PIF file	Program information file - gives information to Windows about an MS-DOS application.
Pixel	A picture element on screen; the smallest element that can be independently assigned colour and intensity.
Plug-and-play	Hardware which can be plugged into a PC and be used immediately without configuration.
POP	Post Office Protocol - a method of storing and returning e-mail.
Port	The place where information goes into or out of a computer, e.g. a

Glossary of Terms

	modem might be connected to the serial port.
PPP	Point-to-Point Protocol - One of two methods (see SLIP) for using special software to establish a temporary direct connection to the Internet over regular phone lines.
Print queue	A list of print jobs waiting to be sent to a printer.
Program	A set of instructions which cause a computer to perform tasks.
Protocol	A set of rules or standards that define how computers communicate with each other.
Query	The set of keywords and operators sent by a user to a search engine, or a database search request.
Queue	A list of e-mail messages waiting to be sent over the Internet.
RAM	Random Access Memory. The computer's volatile memory. Data held in it is lost when power is switched off.
Real mode	MS-DOS mode, typically used to run programs, such as MS-DOS games, that will not run under Windows.
Resource	A directory, or printer, that can be shared over a network.
Robot	A Web agent that visits sites, by requesting documents from them, for the purposes of indexing for search engines. Also known as Wanderers, Crawlers, or Spiders.
ROM	Read Only Memory. A PC's non-volatile memory. Data is written

Glossary of Terms

	into this memory at manufacture and is not affected by power loss.
Scroll bar	A bar that appears at the right side or bottom edge of a window.
Search	Submit a query to a search engine.
Search engine	A program that helps users find information across the Internet.
Serial interface	An interface that transfers data as individual bits.
Server	A computer system that manages and delivers information for client computers.
Shared resource	Any device, program or file that is available to network users.
Shareware	Software that is available on public networks and bulletin boards. Users are expected to pay a nominal amount to the software developer.
Signature file	An ASCII text file, maintained within e-mail programs, that contains text for your signature.
Site	A place on the Internet. Every Web page has a location where it resides which is called its site.
SLIP	Serial Line Internet Protocol, a method of Internet connection that enables computers to use phone lines and a modem to connect to the Internet without having to connect to a host.
SMTP	Simple Mail Transfer Protocol - a protocol dictating how e-mail messages are exchanged over the Internet.

Glossary of Terms 11

Socket	An endpoint for sending and receiving data between computers.
Software	The programs and instructions that control your PC.
Spamming	Sending the same message to a large number of mailing lists or newsgroups. Also to overload a Web page with excessive keywords in an attempt to get a better search ranking.
Spider	See robot.
Spooler	Software which handles transfer of information to a store to be used by a peripheral device.
SQL	Structured Query Language, used with relational databases.
SSL	Secure Sockets Layer, the standard transmission security protocol developed by Netscape, which has been put into the public domain.
Subscribe	To become a member of.
Surfing	The process of looking around the Internet.
SVGA	Super Video Graphics Array; it has all the VGA modes but with 256, or more, colours.
Swap file	An area of your hard disc used to store temporary operating files, also known as virtual memory.
Sysop	System Operator - A person responsible for the physical operations of a computer system or network resource.

11 Glossary of Terms

System disc	A disc containing files to enable a PC to start up.
T1	An Internet leased line that carries up to 1.536 million bits per second (1.536Mbps).
T3	An Internet leased line that carries up to 45 million bits per second (45Mbps).
TCP/IP	Transmission Control Protocol/Internet Protocol, combined protocols that perform the transfer of data between two computers. TCP monitors and ensures the correct transfer of data. IP receives the data, breaks it up into packets, and sends it to a network within the Internet.
Telnet	A program which allows people to remotely use computers across networks.
Text file	An unformatted file of text characters saved in ASCII format.
Thread	An ongoing message-based conversation on a single subject.
TIFF	Tag Image File Format - a popular graphic image file format.
Tool	Software program used to support Web site creation and management.
Toolbar	A bar containing icons giving quick access to commands.
Toggle	To turn an action on and off with the same switch.
TrueType fonts	Fonts that can be scaled to any size and print as they show on the screen.

Glossary of Terms

UNC	Universal Naming Convention - A convention for files that provides a machine independent means of locating the file that is particularly useful in Web based applications.
UNIX	Multitasking, multi-user computer operating system that is run by many computers that are connected to the Internet.
Upload/Download	The process of transferring files between computers. Files are uploaded from your computer to another and downloaded from another computer to your own.
URL	Uniform Resource Locator, the addressing system used on the Web, containing information about the method of access, the server to be accessed and the path of the file to be accessed.
Usenet	Informal network of computers that allow the posting and reading of messages in newsgroups that focus on specific topics.
User ID	The unique identifier, usually used in conjunction with a password, which identifies you on a computer.
Virtual Reality	Simulations of real or imaginary worlds, rendered on a flat two-dimensional screen but appearing three-dimensional.
Virus	A malicious program, downloaded from a web site or disc, designed to wipe out information on your computer.

11 Glossary of Terms

W3C	The World Wide Web Consortium that is steering standards development for the Web.
WAIS	Wide Area Information Server, a Net-wide system for looking up specific information in Internet databases.
WAV	Waveform Audio (.wav) - a common audio file format for DOS/Windows computers.
Web	A network of hypertext-based multimedia information servers. Browsers are used to view any information on the Web.
Web Page	An HTML document that is accessible on the Web.
Webmaster	One whose job it is to manage a web site.
WINSOCK	A Microsoft Windows file that provides the interface to TCP/IP services.
Wizard	A Microsoft tool that asks you questions and then creates an object depending on your answers.

Appendix A

Keyboard Shortcuts

The following keyboard actions are the standard shortcuts for working with Internet Explorer 5 and Outlook Express 5.

Keyboard Shortcuts for Explorer 5

Shortcut   *Action*

Viewing Web Pages

Shortcut	Action
F1	Open Explorer Help
F11	Toggle fullscreen view
Tab	Move forward through object items
Sh+Tab	Move backward through object items
Alt+Home	Go to Home page
Alt+>	Go to the next page
Alt+<	Go to the previous page
Sh+F10	Display shortcut menu for link
F6	Move forward between frames
Sh+Ctrl+Tab	Move back between frames
↑	Scroll up a document
↓	Scroll down a document
PgUp	Large scroll up a document
PgDn	Large scroll down a document
Home	Move to the beginning of a document
End	Move to the end of a document
Ctrl+F	Find on this page
F5	Refresh Web page if necessary
Ctrl+F5	Refresh Web page if necessary or not
Esc	Stop downloading a page
Ctrl+O	Go to a new location
Ctrl+N	Open a new window
Ctrl+W	Close the current window

Appendix A - Keyboard Shortcuts

Shortcut	*Action*
Ctrl+S	Save the current page
Ctrl+P	Print the current page or active frame
Enter	Activate a selected link
Ctrl+E	Open Search in Explorer bar
Ctrl+I	Open Favorites in Explorer bar
Ctrl+H	Open History in Explorer bar
Ctrl+click	Open multiple folders (History/Favorites)

Using the Address bar

Alt+D	Select text in the Address bar
F4	Display Address bar history
Ctrl+<	Move cursor left to next '.' or '/'
Ctrl+>	Move cursor right to next '.' or '/'
Ctrl+Enter	Add 'www.' and '.com' to typed text
↑	Move up AutoComplete list
↓	Move down AutoComplete list

Working with Favorites

Ctrl+D	Add page to Favorites
Ctrl+B	Open Organize Favorites box
Alt+↑	Move item up Favorites list
Alt+↓	Move item down Favorites list

Editing

Ctrl+X	Cut to the Clipboard
Ctrl+C	Copy to the Clipboard
Ctrl+V	Insert Clipboard contents
Ctrl+A	Select all items on Web page

Keyboard Shortcuts for Outlook Express 5

Shortcut   *Action*

General

F1	Open help topics
Ctrl+A	Select all messages

Main Mail Window

Ctrl+O	Open the selected message
Ctrl+Q	Mark a message as read
Tab	Move between window panes

Main and Read Message Windows

Ctrl+D	Delete a message
Ctrl+F	Forward a message
Ctrl+I	Go to your Inbox
Ctrl+M	Send and receive mail
Ctrl+N	Open a new message
Ctrl+P	Print the selected message
Ctrl+R	Reply to the message author
Sh+Ctrl+R	Reply to all
Ctrl+U	Go to next unread message
Ctrl+>	Go to next message in the list
Ctrl+<	Go to previous message in the list
Alt+Enter	View properties of selected message
Sh+Ctrl+B	Open Address Book
Ctrl+Y	Go to folder

New Message Window

F3	Find text
F7	Check spelling
Esc	Close a message
Ctrl+K	Check names
Ctrl+Enter	Send a message
Sh+Ctrl+S	Add a signature
Alt+S	Send a message

Appendix A - Keyboard Shortcuts

Shortcut   *Action*

Main News Window

Sh+Ctrl+A	Mark all news messages as read
Ctrl+J	Go to next unread newsgroup
Sh+Ctrl+M	Download news for offline reading
Ctrl+O	Open the selected message
Ctrl+Q	Mark a message as read
Ctrl+W	Go to a newsgroup
Ctrl+Y	Go to a folder
Tab	Move between window panes
← or **+**	Expand a news thread
→ or **-**	Collapse a news thread

Main and Read Message Windows

F5	Refresh headers and articles
Ctrl+F	Forward a message
Ctrl+G	Reply to all
Ctrl+N	Post new message to the newsgroup
Ctrl+P	Print the selected message
Ctrl+R	Reply to the author
Ctrl+>	Go to the next message in the list
Ctrl+<	Go to previous message in the list
Alt+Enter	View properties of selected message
Sh+Ctrl+U	Go to next unread conversation

New Message Window

Sh+Ctrl+F	Find text
Esc	Close a message
Ctrl+K	Check names
Alt+S	Send a message
F7	Check spelling

Appendix B

Internet File Formats

All of the file formats found on the Internet can be broken into one of two types: **ASCII** text files you can view with WordPad or Notepad, and **Binary** which contain non-ASCII characters and cannot be viewed.

We include here a guide to the most common Internet file formats with details of how some of them can be viewed, or played.

Plain Text (ASCII) Files

.html/.htm The language in which Web documents are authored. File type is ASCII and requires a Web browser like Explorer for viewing.

.txt An ASCII text file which can be viewed with Notepad.

Formatted Documents

.doc Used for formatted ASCII text files, but also for documents created in Microsoft Word.

.pdf Portable Document Format, a binary format developed by Adobe Systems Inc., that allows formatted documents to be transferred across the Internet so they look the same on any machine. Requires a Reader which is freely available directly from Adobe.

Appendix B - Internet File Formats

.ps — A PostScript file is unreadable except by a PostScript printer, or with an onscreen viewer like GhostScript.

Compressed and Encoded Files

.arc — An old binary format for archiving and compression, which can be manipulated by several programs, but especially ZipMagic.

.arj — A binary format for MS-DOS machines, especially in Europe. You can use WinZIP, or ZipMagic.

.bin — A Macbinary II Encoded File requiring Stuffit Expander.

.exe — A DOS or Windows binary executable program or self-extracting file. Launched by double-clicking on the file's icon.

.gz/gzip — The GNU Project's compression program, a binary format most commonly used for UNIX and PC files. Use ZipMagic which handles this format the same way as Zip files.

.hqx — A Macintosh binary file that has been converted into ASCII text so it can be safely transferred across the Net. Use BinHex13 (binhex13.zip) on a Windows PC to un-binhex it.

.sit — A Macintosh binary file that has been compressed using the Stuffit program. Use Stuffit Expander for Windows.

.sea — A Macintosh self-extracting binary archive file.

.tar/.tar.gz/.tar.Z/.tgz

These binary files are often found on Unix-based Internet sites. ZipMagic handles all these formats the same way as Zip files.

.uu UUencoded binary file. Used to convert binary data into text so it can be sent via e-mail. Explorer automatically decodes this type. You can also use WinCode to UUdecode files in Windows.

.Z A UNIX binary compression format. Use ZipMagic to decompress and view files with this extension.

.zip A common binary compression standard for DOS and Windows that uses the DOS utility PKZIP. These files can be decompressed on the PC with WinZIP, or ZipMagic.

Graphics Files

.gif One of the most common graphics file formats on the Internet, it stands for Graphics Interchange Format. Explorer views these automatically.

.jpg/.jpeg A popular binary compression standard used for photos and still images. Explorer also views these automatically.

.tiff/.tif A very large, high-resolution binary image format. You can use Lview Pro or PolyView on a Windows PC.

Appendix B - Internet File Formats

Sound Files

.au/uLaw/MuLaw
: The most common sound format (binary) found on the Web.

.aiff/.aif
: A fairly common Macintosh sound format found on the Web.

.mid/ .rmi
: Musical Instrument Digital Interface files.

.ra
: Real Audio, a new binary audio format, which allows you to play sounds in real-time.

.wav
: Audio for Windows, the native sound format for Windows.

Video Files

.avi
: Audio Visual Interleave, the standard binary video format for Windows.

.mov/.qt
: Common binary formats for QuickTime movies, the Macintosh native movie platform.

.mpg/mpeg
: A standard binary format for 'movies' on the Internet, using the MPEG compression scheme. There is an MPEG FTP Site that has a large collection of MPEG player resources for all platforms (Mac, Windows, and UNIX).

.ra/ .ram/ .rm/ .rmm
: RealNetworks, RealAudio, and RealVideo files.

All of these multimedia file types can be played by the Microsoft Windows Media Player, that was released at the same time as Windows 98.

Index

Acronyms 119
Adding
    attachments 99
    Favorite 70
    Favorite folder 73
    news server 124
Address
    bar 21, 30
    Book 109
Addresses
    e-mail 82
    URL 7
alt groups 122, 130
Archive file 44
ARPANET 2
Assistant, Search 59
Attachments 94, 99
Autocomplete 30
Autosearch 31

Bar
    Address 21, 30
    Explorer 23, 51
    Links 32
    Menu 22
    Radio 23
    Status 19, 23
    Title 22
Behaviour 137
Blocking senders 114
Bookmarks 69
Browser 5, 58

Caches 53, 134
CD-ROM 12

Censored viewing 141
Checking
    mail 88
    spelling 104
Colour control 34
Command button 22
Connection
    Outlook Express 106
    to Internet 11
    to server 84
Contacts pane 90
Control bars 29
Copying text 41
Customise
    Search Assistant 60
    Toolbar 28

Deja.com 66
Deleted Items folder ... 102
Document source 42
Domain 7
Download
    file 45
    page 43
Drafts folder 102
Drag toolbar 29

E-mail 4, 81
    addresses 82
    address book 109
    attachments 94, 99
    deleting 101
    folders 102
    formatting 98
    header 88

171

Index

printing 107
removing 101
sending 89, 100
subject 88
symbols 119
toolbar 92
window layout 87, 89
Enable ratings 141
Engines, search 61
Etiquette 139
Explorer
bar 23, 51
download site 12
Help 36
installing 12
products 10
requirements 10
screen layout 21
security 54
starting 14
versions 10

Favorites 69
adding 70
folders 69, 73
framed pages 74
Links bar 74
menu 69
offline 75
organising 72
properties 79
using 71
window 72
File
attachments 94, 99
formats 167
printing 48
properties 47
transfers 5
signature 97
Filtering messages 112

Finding
e-mail address 92
mail list 117
Web sites 59
Flaming 137
Folder
Favorites 69, 73
maintenance 72
system 102
temporary 46
Folders List 89
Font control 34
Format
message 98
toolbar 99
Frame printing 49
Free browsers 9
FTP 5
Fullscreen view 32

General option settings . 33
Getting
browser 12
online 11
Glossary 143
Go button 21, 62
Gopher 8
Graphics 35, 130, 169

Header pane 126
Help
Address Book 111
Explorer 36
Outlook Express 103
History files 51
Hotmail 115
HTML format 7, 98
Hypermedia 6
Hypertext links 6

Inbox folder 102

Index

Information Super Highway 4
Installing Explorer 12
Internet 1
   access 11
   behaviour 137
   Connection Wizard 14, 84
   etiquette 139
   file formats 167
   flames 137
   history 1
   provider 11
   Service Provider ... 8, 11
   software source 47
   uses 4

Junk mail 114

Keyboard shortcuts . 25, 163

Link
   names 7
   printing 50
   saving 42
Links 6, 19
Links Bar 32
List
   Blocked Senders ... 114
   Folders 89
   mailing 117
   Message 90
   sorting 90
Live radio 23
Long distance computing . 5

Mail
   Folders List 89
   toolbar 92
   window 89
Mailbox 81, 89
Mailing lists 117
Main window 89

Menu bar 22
   options 24
Message
   attachments 94, 99
   filtering 112
   formatting 98
   List 90
   New window 94
   organise 101
   priority 90
   Read window 93
   Remove deleted 101
   reply to 100, 129
   Rules 112
   sorting 127
   Stationery 95
   status icons 91, 132
   threaded 132
MIME 99
Modem 10
Mouse
   pointer 41
   right-click menu 25

Netiquette 139
Networks 11
New
   components 58
   window 20
New Message
   toolbar 96
   window 94
News 121
   server 123
   settings 123
   toolbar 128
   window 127
Newsgroups 5, 66, 122
   searching 66
   window 125

173

Index

Offline
  Favorites 75
  viewing 75, 133
Online
  getting 11
  tutorial 38
Opening
  Explorer 14
  Outlook Express 84
  new window 20
Option settings 33
Organise messages ... 101
Outbox folder 89, 102
Outlook Express ... 81, 121
Own signature 97

Page saving 43
PC settings 16
Pictures 35, 130, 169
Pixels 16
Plain text 98
Preview
  pane 91
  print 50
Priorities 90
Printing 48, 107
Properties
  Favorites 79
  file 47

Radio 23
Rating system 142
Read Message
  toolbar 93
  window 93, 129
Refresh page 54
Removing messages .. 101
Replying
  e-mail 100
  news message 129
Right-clicking 25

Rules, message 112

Saving
  e-mail attachments ... 94
  file 45
  links 42
  page 43
  pictures 35
  Web archive 44
  with graphics 43
  whole pages 43
Screen
  layout 21
  resolution 16
Scroll controls 23
Search
  Assistant 59
  button 17, 59
  engines 61
  tools 17, 61
Secure transaction 56
Security 54
  zones 55
Selecting text 41
Sending e-mail 89, 100
Sent Items folder 102
Server
  connecting to 84
  News 123
Settings 16, 33
Shortcuts 25, 163
Signature 97
Smileys 119
Software source 47
Sorting messages 127
Sound files 170
Source code 42
Spam 138
Spelling check 104
Standard Toolbar 26
Start (home) page ... 15, 39

174

Index

Starting
   Explorer 14
   Outlook Express 84
Stationery 95
Status
   bar 19, 23
   icons 91, 132
   indicator 23
Subscribing
   to mailing list 118
   to newsgroup 126
Super Highway 4
Surfing 4
Symbols 119
Synchronization 77
System folders 102

TCP/IP protocol 3
Telnet 8
Temporary folder 46
Text file 44, 167
Threaded messages .. 132
Title bar 22
Toolbar
   customise 28
   e-mail format 99
   Explorer window 26
   layout 29
   Mail Main window 92
   New Message 96
   News 128
   News window 128
   Read Message 93
   Standard 26
Trial run 17, 88
Tucows 47
Tutorial, online 38

URL addressing 7, 30
Useful site 40
Usenet 121

newsgroups .. 5, 66, 122
types 138

Video files 170
Viewing
   file attachments 94
   fullscreen 32
   offline 133
   source code 42

WAIS 8
Web
   archive 44
   information 40
   language 7
   tutorials 38
Window
   buttons 22
   Main 89
   new 20
   New Message 94
   News 127
   Read Message .. 93, 129
World Wide Web 5

Yahoo 65

Notes

Companion Discs

COMPANION DISCS are available for most computer books written by the same author(s) and published by BERNARD BABANI (publishing) LTD, as listed at the front of this book (except for those marked with an asterisk).

There is no Companion Disc for this book

To obtain companion discs for other books, fill in the order form below, or a copy of it, enclose a cheque (payable to **P.R.M. Oliver**) or a postal order, and send it to the address given below. **Make sure you fill in your name and address** and specify the book number and title in your order.

Book No.	**Book Name**	**Unit Price**	**Total Price**
BP		£3.50	
BP		£3.50	
BP		£3.50	
Name .... Address		Sub-total £............. P & P (@ 45p/disc) £............. Total Due £.............	
Send to: P.R.M. Oliver, CSM, Pool, Redruth, Cornwall, TR15 3SE			

PLEASE NOTE

The author(s) are fully responsible for providing this Companion Disc service. The publishers of this book accept no responsibility for the supply, quality, or magnetic contents of the disc, or in respect of any damage, or injury that might be suffered or caused by its use.

Notes